PUBLIC ENTERPRISES MANAGEMENT

PUBLIC ENTERPRISES MANAGEMENT

Issues and Perspective

By

R.K. MISHRA

P. GEETA ● B. NAVIN

ANMOL PUBLICATIONS PVT. LTD.

NEW DELHI - 110 002 (INDIA)

ANMOL PUBLICATIONS PVT. LTD.
4374/4B, Ansari Road, Daryaganj
New Delhi - 110 002
www.anmolbooks.com

Public Enterprises Management: Issues and Perspective

First Edition, 2002

ISBN 81-261-1021-X

PRINTED IN INDIA

Published by J.L. Kumar for Anmol Publications Pvt. Ltd., New Delhi - 110 002 and Printed at Mehra Offset Press, Delhi.

Contents

Preface

The constellation of global economic forces acting upon the various economic and business entities in a transforming economy such as India necessitates a thorough inquiry into its major dimensions. This book is an attempt to capture the salient features of such major issues. Chapter 1 outlines the leading issues relating to public enterprises. Government policies with respect to disinvestment, turning around sick units, privatization, wage revision and MoU's as a tool have been highlighted in this chapter. The second chapter discusses the problems in the disinvestment process at the policy and operational levels. Chapter 3 assesses the disinvestment experiments of late 90's with a view to facilitate planning of fast track disinvestment exercise for the future by drawing upon lessons from the past.

Chapter 4 focuses on the various implementing agencies in the disinvestment process. It brings out the cumbersome, Multilayered and non-conducive nature of the disinvestment. Chapter 5 provides a comprehensive background to memorandum of understanding of in India. It traces out the development of MoU as a tool in the public enterprise management right from its inception to its present stage. It also brings out the extent of academic research conducted so far in this area. Chapter 7 analyses the competitiveness of public sector in India. It discusses the significance of competitiveness in public sector To the Indian economy: its present orientation with regard competitiveness, status of its competitiveness and measures to make it internationally competitive. Chapter 8 describes the productivity scenario in public enterprises on the basis of parameters such as profitability, value added, capital productivity and output. Chapter 9 deals with MoU in India while Financial autonomy and accountability of public enterprises is analysed in Chapter 10. Financial administration of public enterprises is given competent treatment in the concluding chapter.

The book on the whole attempts to bring together, the manifold dimensions of critical issues at the policy and operational levels of the Indian public enterprise management process.

1

Some Recent Issues Relating to Public Enterprises

— *R.K. Mishra*

The onset of economic reforms in July 1991 unleashed thoughtless attacks on public enterprise. The champions of private sector sitting round the corner waiting for an opportunity were elated and pumped in all their energies to utilise the public sector wealth that could give a quantum jump to their unaccounted assets, to boost their exploitative socio-economic-political power. The buzz words globalisation and internationalisation equipped them with dangerous arsenal to announce their victory. Since then the unchanged face of first the minority and then the continuing coalition politics has caused irreparable damage to these enterprises. The year 1998-99 and the period till date have seen the situation worsening. The Minister for Industry in his inaugural address at the seminar on restructuring public sector organised by FICCI on July 5, 1999 said that investments in public enterprise will depend on their financial performance which in his view is to get a shot in the arm by the restructuring measures that have been initiated by the Government. On an investment of Rs. 2,50,000 crore in 1998-99, these enterprises have earned a net profit of Rs. 30,000 crore, which is more than 10% on the funds deployed. The special survey published in June, 1999 carried out by the Centre for Monitoring Indian Economy compares the public-private sector performance. The survey brings out very forcefully the fact that an inefficient private sector in terms of financial profitability of less than 10% cannot accuse its counterpart of sub-optimal performance to stake the claim of dismantling the public sector and write *ab initio,* a new equation for economic development. Some of the major developments related to public enterprises in 1998-99 reinforce our belief that Government's move with regard to public enterprises were not performance based but were motivated to satisfy the promoters of crony capitalism.

Disinvestment

The NDA Government proposes to employ disinvestments in public sector as a strategic tool to restructure the national finances in order to revitalise the Indian economy. It is essential at this juncture to assess the disinvestment experience of 1998-99 to draw suitable lessons to place the disinvestment exercise on the fast track for 1999-2000.

In 1998-99, the different heads of the Government spoke in different voices showing that there was hardly any coordination in their thinking displaying their utter disregard to the fact that they were organs of the same body. They embarrassed themselves often by making contradictory statements. Their casual approach gave a world-wide impression of the lack of professionalism and will to learn from the global experiences. The policy makers exhibited their inability to see the big picture of the problem as they reflected the limitation of their intellect to see the problem at the best in some parts which probably could best sub-serve the interest of their client groups.

It was argued that the formation of the trust would rid public enterprises of the Government control and provide an ease of action to sell the share holdings transferred to fill back the Government coffers. The Government officials in the best traditions of the civil service saw the impending danger of losing control on public enterprises and using them as whipping boys. The Finance Secretary to the Government of India, hard pressed to mitigate the fiscal deficit, introduced a new concept.

The special purpose vehicle as per the Finances Secretary's views, was the best way to put disinvestment programme on the fast track and achieve the initial target of Rs. 5,000 Crore set for the year 1998-99. According to this concept, a special purpose vehicle (SPV) with a limited capital investment (it is said that there are 30,000 SPVs with an average capital of Rs. 10,000 each) was to be set up to which the share capital of the enterprises to be disinvested was to be transferred. The SPV in return would approach the financial institutions/capital markets to pay back the money to the Government against the equities off loaded by the Government. Another concept suggested was that of the 'warehousing' which meant sale of shares to the financial institutions for the purposes of realisation of equity values and keeping such shares in bank vaults as long as they could not realise the best value. The Unit Trust of India (UTI), the biggest mutual fund as also the biggest buyer of public sector shares, stung by its failure of efficiently managing US 1964, was not ready to accept the generous invitation of the Government lest it crumbled and to take the last breath. The other financial institutions sensing the ultimate danger joined the UTI and refused to tiptoe the Government. The failure of the disinvestment programme of the highly financially successful enterprise, Container Corporation of India Limited (CONCOR), which had earlier pitched the sale of shares at Rs. 450 per share and had to climb down later to agree to a price of Rs. 225-230 per share shook the other enterprises which were to disinvest their shareholdings including the Oil and Natural Gas Company Limited (ONGC) and the Indian Petro Chemicals Limited. The financial institutions seeing virtue in the CONCOR shareholdings picked up the disinvested stake only to realise that the shares of trading in the range of Rs. 210-180 undermining their capitalisation. The Government had fixed a target of realising Rs. 5000 crore from disinvestment in 1998-99 which was revised later to Rs. 9000 crore. The Government realised Rs. 6190 crore as on March 31, 1999 (Table 1.1). The bulk of this amount of Rs. 6190 crore was realised through the controversial cross holdings. Having succeeded in this, the Finance Minister set a target of Rs. 10,000 crore for disinvestments for 1999-2000. The

IOC, GAIL, MRL, MTNL, VSNL, HZL and ITDC shareholdings are slated to be on block in 1999-2000.

The increasing fiscal deficits, left no choice for the policy makers and the Finance Minister and the Finance Secretary but to have a greater reliance on disinvestments of the shareholdings of the public enterprises. This led to the innovation of 'buy back of shares' which implied acquisition of the Government shareholdings by the cash rich enterprises. This obviously worked in the favour of the Government but turned out to be a huge dent in the cash flow of the disinvested enterprises affecting the tempo of their investments in R & D, expansion and maintenance. This also worked at cross purposes with the Government's new economic policy initiative of making public enterprises gain in terms of size and operations. To net more proceeds from this process, the Finance Ministry suggested the public sector oil enterprises to give effect to cross shareholdings in their equities which could benefit the Government on the one hand and the public sector oil enterprises on the other by enhancing coordination and integration of upstream and downstream operations and may also offer the advantages of economies of scale. Some common directors on the Board of such companies were introduced apparently to defend the concept. However, only the future will tell as to whether the so called advantages materialise or not. Nonethe less, the Government has succeeded in making public enterprises worse off by the cross holding investments as it has realised the money arising out of such transactions. The oil companies in the public sector picked up for the cross holdings instead of becoming globai giants are faced with cash crunch explaining in more than one words about the lack of justification for this method of disinvestment employed by the Government. The IOC-ONGC swap hit price hitch with both companies settling for a pricing following which the stock prices fell by at least fifteen to twenty per cent.

The erstwhile Disinvestment Commission went ahead with its work. It submitted twelve reports during its tenure covering 58 enterprises. The Commission's recommendations in general did not find favour with the Government. The Chairman of the Commission and some of its members threatened to quit the Commission. The

Commission did not make any impact as it continued to be an executive body manned both at the top and at the administrative level by bureaucrats. Its members though eminent had not had significant interface with disinvestments earlier. The Commission did not develop any database in the absence of which its recommendations missed the requisite research back up. The Government dilly-dallied the appointment of its members and extension of tenure. It will be in the fitness of things that the process of disinvestment should be left to the concerned enterprises which could carefully examine the matters such as readying themselves for disinvestments, preparing their own calendars for disinvestment exercise, timing and pricing of shareholdings and extent of their disinvestment.

If disinvestments have to be used as a technique of restructuring of public enterprises, the time is ripe for the Government to give a fresh look towards its objectives of disinvestment. The financing of fiscal deficit should be relegated to much lower place in order as compared to upgradation of technology and provision of safety net as the objectives of disinvestment. Sadly, all that Government has done in the realm of disinvestments has been nothing more than implementing the programme only in letter and missing in its spirit centpercent. Hardly any consideration has been given to readying public enterprises for disinvestments. In a nutshell the programme has jumped straight from a naught to nine without caring for the intervening steps. The process of introducing user charges, commercialisation and corporatisation has been thrown to wind. The results are for any one to see. The share prices of the listed public enterprises over a period of one year shown a steep decline in the case of Steel Authority of India Limited, Bharat Earth Movers Limited, Indian Petro Chemicals Limited, Indian Telephone Industries, Balmer Lawrie Limited and its associate Balmer Lawrie-Van Leer to mention a few. The market has taken note of the Government's unwillingness to withdraw from public enterprise and remove the sinister shadow of civil servants and discounted any hope for future as the Government and its civil service have discredited practically every important move to reform.

Board for Industrial and Financial Reconstruction (BIFR) — Turning Around Sick Units

The Government has refused to recognise the special characteristics of sickness in public enterprises and has put in place the same route as prescribed for private sector in the form of BIFR. This has taken a long time for the Government to understand the problem of sickness in public enterprises and still a far longer time for the BIFR to prepare rehabilitation plans even for a few public enterprises. The rehabilitation plan for the Indian Drugs & Pharmaceuticals Limited (IDPL) and the Nagaland Pulp and Paper Company Limited are cases in point. The Government has cold shouldered the suggestion of setting up a special bench in BIFR to expedite the cases from public enterprises registered with it. Inordinate delays in taking up the cases for hearing and the lack of expertise hampered the formulation of rehabilitation packages and turnaround of sick public enterprises. One of the reasons for the rehabilitation schemes becoming suspect is the lack of their financial credibility. The central cabinet in October 1998, approved a proposal to shut down Mining and Allied Machinery Corporation, Cycle Corporation of India, National Instrumentation Limited, Weighburd India, Rehabilitation Industries Corporation, Tanneries and Footwear Corporation, Bharat Opthalmic Glass Limited and National Bicycle Corporation. The VRS for 11,000 workers in these enterprises was to cost the national exchequer Rs. 517 crore. The revival costs were estimated at Rs. 400 crore only. This was certainly bad economics. Weighburd India could be revived at the cost of Rs. 3.2 crore, while the cost of VRS was in the region of Rs. 15-20 crore. The revival scheme of Bharat Opthalmic would cost Rs. 20 crore while the cost of VRS was Rs. 25 crore. The Government can now at least start seeing virtue in turnaround through rehabilitation.

Privatisation

For the first time in the 1999-2000 Budget presented to the Indian Parliament, the Finance Minister conceded that the Government was using cold privatisation as the technique of restructuring. However, it was not content with the results and that it will resort to direct techniques of privatisation in future. But the

Government has never made it clear as to who would take over the privatised enterprises. In our view, the economy will fail to benefit by the transfer of a sick public enterprise to an inefficient private enterprise. Further the resource position of the country will not improve and the attendant spurt in employment, savings and investments is not likely to occur as long as the foreign buyers do bring in the risk capital. The Government's existing approach of asking the ministries/concerned enterprises or the Disinvestment Commission to appoint global advisor to rope in strategic buyer's optimism about infusing foreign funds. On the contrary, it may result in a net cash outgo by way of the payment of huge fee and dividends. It may also result in affecting the foreign exchange position on both the capital and current account specially under the present circumstances in which portfolio investments constitute an important component of the FDIs. Although the Government emphasis the need for setting up a comprehensive social safety net, the progress has been tardy as the employees grouse of making the VRS attractive has fallen on its deaf ears. Government has admitted non-capability to introduce the Employment Insurance Scheme and a comprehensive net work of retraining and re-employment institutions. Despite an open stand on privatisation, the public sector's contribution in total industrial production continues to remain very high as seen from Table 1.2. The Government presented the bill for the privatisation of insurance in the parliament based on the recommendations of the Malhotra Committee Report and to comply with the fiats of the World Trade Organisation to open up the financial sector by 2003. Apart from the pro-privatisation lobby, comprising the Chambers of Commerce and Industry, foreign business interests, foreign government delegations as well as foreign insurance companies, constantly urged the Government to open up the sector. The move attracted a scrious opposition and due to popular public pressure, the Government could not push through the bill. The Government having failed in its first attempt, tried to manoeuvre its coalition partners and some opposition parties once again. However, due to dissension with the coalition, and later due to its fall, the insurance bill could not take off. Interestingly, the tie-ups proposed for the insurance sector had their business focus solely on non-life products. The tie-ups are silent on crop insurance. They have not stated their position on the coverage of various risks that afflict Indian industry from time to time. It is a moot point to consider whether we should privatise our insurance industry this way? Table 1.3 provides details on tie-ups in the insurance sector.

Privatisation and regulation are two sides of the same coin. The experience with the British and French privatisation shows that unregulated privatisation may result in the decline of social welfare. The Insurance Regulatory Authority Act passed in 1998, awaits its implementation in the form of the Insurance Regulatory Authority. As a part of power sector reforms, the Central Government has set up the Central Electricity Regulatory Authority and some State Governments tempted by the financial incentives provided by the Power Finance Corporation, have set up the State Electricity Regulatory Commissions. The experience in regulation pertaining to the Telephone Regulatory Authority of India Limited (TRAI), casts doubts about the respect that the State should have for such autonomous regulatory bodies and also the approach that should be followed by the regulatory bodies. For instance, the regulatory bodies, in principle, have accepted the approach of the Central and the State Governments towards reforming the power sector which is a stereotype of the World Bank approach resting on the supply side ignoring completely the demand side of the equation. Such an approach has benefited rich countries on the globe such as the USA, France, UK and Australia; MNCs such as ENRON among business enterprises and opportunist business groups such as Hindujas and GVK Groups.

Wage Revision

While accepting the Mohan Committee Report on wage revision in public enterprises, the Government left it to each and every public enterprise to examine its paying capacity to meet the burden arising out of its implementation. The Government has categorised public enterprise into 3 divisions: public enterprises earning profits continuously for three years; public enterprises recording mixed performance; and public enterprises suffering from sickness. The enterprises consistently earning profits could implement the revision, the mixed performance enterprises are required to take the approval of the respective ministries and the sick enterprises have to get the burden of implementation incorporated in the rehabilitation packages. The Government's apathy to justify demands for wage revision in public enterprises can be seen from the fact that there has been no wage revision for the last 13 years in the Mining and Allied Machinery Corporation which has a workforce of 5000.

The Government has glossed over the real problem of ensuring the payment of revised wages to the personnel of loss making and sick public enterprises. The wages and incentives account for approximately 10% of the cost of production. Experience shows that the productivity in public enterprises is positively related to the offering of incentives. But this is seldom allowed to happen as is evidenced in the case of the Goa Shipyard Limited whose management had to pay a price for introducing an enterprise specific incentive scheme.

MoU as a Tool

The MoU was introduced to iron out the conflict between the accountability and autonomy. However, the expected results have not fructified. On the part of the Government, its lack of will to provide due support to public enterprises in order to enable them the various targets set for the financial year has come in the way of the success of the MoU system. On the part of public enterprise, their lack of sincerity reflected by their lack of will to share the relevant information has failed this new instrument. Though, a large number of public enterprises have been awarded 'A' grade subsequent to the fulfilment of targets set out in MoUs, the total factor productivity has not registered any noticeable change. The initiation of measures such as Navaratnas and Miniratnas have also fallen short of expectations as the good intentions of the Department of Public Enterprise have been countered more than once by the concerned administrative ministries. To add to the woes, even the

Navaratna package does not provide any evidence of the Government's intention of loosening its control. The newly constituted Governing Boards of Navaratna enterprises have retired Civil Servants as part-time directors. Some persons have found placed on the Government Boards of more than one Navaratnas. Surprisingly, the Government, even after the announcement of this autonomy measure in 1996 has not been able to complete the process of formation of the Boards by filling up all positions.

According to a study (*Yamuna Krishna, Disinvestments in Public Enterprises, a research completed for Ph.D. Degree in Business Management, Institute of Public Enterprise, Hyderabad, 1999)* the composite score of disinvested units on MoU system has increased marginally during 1991-92 and 1998-99. During 1998-99, while some enterprises had recourse to innovative sources of finance. The Government of India did not clear the financial restructuring plan of the National Aluminum Company Limited and Singareni Collieries Company Limited to mention a few. This increased either the loses or affected the market capitalisation through a lower earnings per share. The Union Cabinet sat over the proposal for the much needed equity induction of Rs. 1000 crore to bail out Air India from its financial crisis which was a must to kick off some of the basics for the disinvestments of Government equity in public enterprises. Its problem included a paid up share capital of Rs. 154 crore which must be pumped up to Rs. 1924 crore by disinvesting an ageing fleet of 26 aircrafts. It is difficult to understand as to why the Government was delaying the clearance of the proposal, especially when a similar proposal by Indian Airlines costing Rs. 325 crore was given a nod. That the Government has not regard to autonomy is seen from the fact that on one fine morning Mr. P.C. Sen, CMD, Indian Airlines was shown the door and the Boards of the two national Air Lines were merged to the dismay of experts. The Air India intended to securities its future earnings to improve its cash flows. It also proposed to reduce its staff per aircraft drastically. The Indian Oil Corporation decided to go in for a Rs. 700 crore Initial Public Offer (IPO) which was to include the private placement tranche. In the name of withdrawal of purchase preference for providing level playing field to private sector, the Government has hit very hard such public enterprises which manufacture intermediate goods and survive on the orders of public enterprises engaged in producing final goods. The Steel Authority of India Limited, a Navaratna, has seen dust because the Indian Railways cancelled its long term orders of buying rail lines from Bhilai Steel Plant and obligate South Korea. The Durgarpur Steel Plant had to virtually close its Axle and Wheel Plant as the Indian Railways curtailed its off take. Similarly power houses were not longer beholden to Bharat Heavy Electricals Limited as several private sector companies and multinational companies have started manufacturing crucial equipment like transformers with foreign technology collaborations.

To conclude, the year 1998-99 was punctuated by the continuous indifference of the Government to public enterprises. Several of its measures affected their performance adversely. Despite this, public enterprises have given a good account of their performance measures in terms of financial profitability vis-a-vis financial profitability of private enterprises. This does not preclude us to suggest that these enterprises should create value for the share holder which impinges upon them to go in for restructuring.

Table 1.1
Disinvestment (Rs. crore)

1995-96		*1996-97*		*1997-98*		*1998-99*	
Target	*Actual*	*Target*	*Actual*	*Target*	*Actual*	*Target*	*Actual*
7000	362	5000	455	7000	906	9000*	6190

*revised

Source: Compiled from Economic Times, February 24 and July 7, 1999.

Table 1.2
Public Sector's Contribution in Total Industrial Production

Item	*Unit*	*National Production*		*Public Sector's Production*		*Percentage of Public Enterprises contribution to National Production*	
		1968-69	*1997-98*	*1968-69*	*1997-98*	*1968-69*	*1997-98*
Fuel							
Coal	Million/Tonnes	71.40	295.93	12.61	289.02	17.66	97.66
Lignite	–do–	3.98	23.05	3.98	23.05	100.00	100.00
Petroleum	–do–	6.06	33.83	3.08	31.35	50.83	92.67
Basic Metal Industries							
Finished Steel	–do–	4.58	22.37	2.55	8.54	55.68	36.54
Non-Ferrous Metals							
Aluminum	Thousand/ Tonnes	125.3	553307	Nil	288360	Nil	52.12
Copper	–do–	9.5	41006	Nil	41006	Nil	100.00
Primary Lead	–do–	1.9	44060	1.9	35766	100.00	81.18
Zinc	–do–	17.0	165000	13.7	136277	80.60	82.59
Fertilisers							
Nitrogenous	–do–	563.0	10085.6	401.0	3340.9	71.23	33.13
Phosphatic	–do–	213.2	2975.4	53.0	728.1	24.86	24.47

Source :Public Enterprise Survey1997-98,Vol.1, p. 9, Department of Public Enterprises, GOI, New Delhi.

Table 1.3
Tie-ups in the Insurance Sector

Indian Partner	*Foreign Partner*	*Country*	*Insurance Business Focus*
Alpic Finance	Allianz	Germany	Non-Life
Tata Group	AIG	US	Non-Life
CK Birla Group	Zurich Insurance	Switzerland	Reinsurance
ICICI	Prudential	UK	Life
Sundaram Finance	Winterhur Ins	Switzerland	
Hindustan Times	Commercial Union	UK	Non-Life
Ranbaxy	Cigna	US	Health (Life)
HDFC	Standard Life	UK	Life
Bombay Dyeing	General Accident	UK	Non-Life
DCM Shriram	Roay Sun Alliance	UK	Non-Life
Dabur	Liberty Mutual	US	
Kotkat Mahindra	Chubb Group	US	Non-Life
Sanmar Group	GIO	Australia	
20th Century Finance	Canada Life	Canada	Life
MA Chidambaram	Metlife	US	

Source: Compiled from *Business Line* (13-7-98) and *Business Standard* (11-12-98 and 7-9-98)

2

What Has Gone Wrong with Disinvestments in Public Enterprises in India?

— *R.K. Mishra*

The purpose of this paper is to provide a brief background of conditions leading to disinvestments in public enterprises (PEs), narrate the progress of disinvestments in PEs since their inception critically examine the measures initiated by the Government to revamp its disinvestment programme, compare the Indian disinvestment scenario with some international experiences, and offer an alternative framework for disinvestments in PEs.

Conditions Leading to Disinvestments

The Indian Government had virtually embraced bankruptcy during the period 1981-1991. Its coffers were empty by the end of this period. The financial condition of the States of the Indian Union was also very critical. This funds crunch forced the Government to incorporate disinvestments as an important element of the New Economic Policy (NEP) announced in July, 1991. The Central Government as well as the State Government had become very weak in terms of political stability by mid-1991. Though sufficient money could have been mopped up through effective mobilisation of excise duties, income tax, sales tax, customs duty, cooperative dues, neither the Central Government nor the State Governments were prepared to opt for this hard measure. There was no preparedness on the part of either the Central Government or the State Governments to prune public expenditure. They preferred to approach the international lending agencies or sell the Government assets. It was realised that dependence on external resources as well as disinvestments had to be resorted to as a measure of political balancing. The political system in India has all through been dominated by the rich and powerful sections of society which do not pay the legitimate taxes and continue to have their stronghold on different institutions of the society. Thus, it was found politically expedient to go in for disinvestments as most of the Government assets since independence, and prior to that period, were built up largely from contributions coming in from the poor sections of society. In order to get a stamp of approval of the economic celebrities, the Government appointed the Krishnamurthy Committee in 1991 and the Rangarajan Committee in 1992. Both the Committees recommended disinvestments to fulfil the objectives of modernisation of the public sector through strengthening R & D, initiating diversification/ expansion programmes, retraining and re-employment of employees, funding the genuine needs of expansion, widening the capital market base, and mitigating fiscal deficits of the Government. These Committees distinguished between the short-term and the long-term goals of disinvestments and advised the Government not to sacrifice the long-term goals for the sake of fulfilling the short-term objectives. However, the Government of India, right from July 1991 economic policy pronouncements to the most recent statement on disinvestments made on July 23, 1998, has consistently stated that mitigating fiscal deficits is the only objective of disinvestments.

Progress and Problems

As shown hereunder 11 rounds of disinvestment has taken place between 1991-92 and 1997-98, yielding Rs. 11,292 crore. Table 2.1 shows the targeted amount of disinvestments was not realised in any fiscal year in this period (except 1991 & 92), and that the average price realisation ratio displayed erratic trends. The procedures adopted for disinvestments suffered from adhocsim. Table 2.1 points out that the contribution of the disinvestment proceeds towards bridging the fiscal deficits was minuscule. and shows the disinvestment modalities recommended and the action actually taken by the Government.

The bundling and bidding were adopted as the first method of disinvestment, subsequently followed by the tendering and the issuance of the global depository receipts (GDR). The auction and public float methods were never used for effecting disinvestments. Initially, the Government placed a number of restrictions as to who could bid for disinvestments, and also put a financial ceiling of Rs. 25 crore for the purchase of disinvested shares. The foreign financial investors were kept out from purchasing the disinvested shares. The Government thought it prudent to allow only the mutual finds to buy the disinvested shares in the first few rounds. The Government advertised for the bids in select national newspapers. The Department of Public Enterprises (DPEs) was the nodal agency to steer the disinvestment process. The Department was empowered to prepare the bundles advertise the bids, select the bidders, finalise the price and effect the disinvestments. An Empowered Committee of Secretaries was appointed to oversee the process of disinvestment effected by DPE. DPE had to furnish the recommendation on behalf of the Committee to the Cabinet Committee on Economic Affairs whose approval was necessary for seeing the transactions through. However, in practice, it was DPE which had a major say. The Empowered Committee turned out to be only an appendage and the Cabinet Committee on Economic Affairs endorsed the recommendations of DPE. A work at the *modus operandi* of DPE with regard to handling the process of disinvestment reveals that the matter was largely dealt with between the then Secretary and a very junior official. The Government in its Statement on the New Economic Policy hinted at selecting suitable PEs for disinvestments. DPE selected 39 enterprises, some of which were profit-making. They belonged to different industrial groups which had varying economic prospects. CMC Limited, which was picked up for disinvestment, had incurred a net loss in 1991. Indian Petro Chemicals Corporation Limited, selected for disinvestment, had bulged profits by adopting inappropriate accounting policies without giving any heed to the norms of sound financial disclosure. DPE put its foot in its mouth by contradicting its own claim that it would realise the best value from disinvestments by pricing the rate of shares on the basis of the peak average values indicated by two out of the three approaches, namely, net asset value method, discounted cash flow method, and the current cost method. Finally, DPE took into consideration the realisations based only on the net assets value method. The Department had no data base. Excepting a couple of officials, its complement of experts did not have economists, engineers and financial experts who were well-versed in the science of disinvestment. The DPE asked the chiefs of PEs/their representatives to sign the proceedings regarding the prices at which shares had to be disinvested, on the dotted lines. It shows that the concerned PE executives had no say in the entire disinvestment process.

Here, it may be pertinent to note that whereas, the international economic community had accumulated much experience on disinvestment by 1991, the policy-makers in India exhibited their lack of knowledge of such experience. The disinvestment process adopted by the Government was not comprehensive. It had narrowly focused only on disinvestment of shareholdings without taking into consideration other important issues such as the initial price offers (IPOs), involvement of strategic partners, introduction of claw-back provision, off loading shares in the capital market book building, setting up a trust of a special purpose vehicle, employees stock ownership and participation, handing over the enterprises to workers' cooperatives/unions and management buy-outs. It also did not touch upon issues such as transfers, mergers and acquisitions. It did not display, at any point of time, its appreciation of the issues related to restructuring of PEs. As per the established international practice, any exercise on disinvestment is preceded by appointment of qualified consultants to advise on the entire process of disinvestment and also help in its implementation. DPE did not profit from this valuable international experience and instead hand picked the Industrial Development Bank of India, SBI Caps, and Industrial Credit & Investment Corporation of India as advisers. Further, scope of their work was limited only to recommending the price at which the shares could be disinvested. However, even these agencies appeared on the scene much later. Initially this role was assigned to

M/s. S. T. Raja Consultants Limited which did not have much relevant experience. Not surprisingly, this hampered realisation of the best price by DPE for them the cash crunch-ridden Central Government. These limitations emerged as a very dominant constraint in the development of the diṣinvestment strategy. They created grave misapprehensions in the mind of the common man in India and led to a severe criticism of the Government on the floor of the Parliament. The popular Indian media raised several issues about the credibility of the entire exercise.

Government's Interventions

The first flash of the Government's mind about the regulation of the disinvestment process was contained in the New Economic Policy Statement of July, 1992. The Government had then stated that an independent legal body was to be constituted to oversee the entire disinvestment process. In 1996, the Government set up the Disinvestment Commission through an executive order. The Government did not legislate on disinvestments, and the Commission's status has remained that of an advisory body. Whose recommendations are not mandatory on the Government. The Commission among other things was asked to:

- — draw a comprehensive overall long-term disinvestment programme within 5-10 years for the
  PSUs referred to it by the Core Group;
- — determine the extent of disinvestment in each of the PSUs;
- — priorities the PSUs referred to it by the Core Group in terms of the overall disinvestment programme;
- — recommend the preferred mode(s) of disinvestment (domestic capital markets/international);
- — capital markets/auction/private sale to identified investors/ any other for each of the identified PSUs;
- — supervise the overall sale process;
- — select the financial advisers;
- — monitor the progress of disinvestment process;

— give wide publicity to the disinvestment proposals; and

— advise the Government on possible capital restructuring.

The Commission has so far brought out ten reports. The Core Group referred 40 enterprises to the commission comprising some Secretaries to the Government of India some of which are common with the enterprises figuring the list of enterprises identified for disinvestments by the Central Government between 1991 and 1996. During 1997-98, three more enterprises, viz, the State Trading Corporation of India Limited, Minerals & Metals Trading Corporation of India Limited, and Project Equipment Construction Limited, have been referred to the Commission.

The Commission has made some general and other enterprise-specific recommendations. Among the general recommendations made, it has given the top slot to improving corporate governance in PEs. The Commission is of the opinion that any disinvestment exercise would not bear the desired fruits as long as the boards of these PEs are not made effective and the Government does not overcome its practice of breathing over the shoulders of these enterprises. The Commission has suggested introduction of sound internal audit, recruitment, materials, MIS, and financial structuring systems. PEs should be transparent in sharing information and in reporting to the investor community.

The Commission has suggested additional autonomy to the moderate performers and near-full autonomy to the best performers. The Commission also suggested setting up of a Pre-investigation Board to save action-oriented chief executives of the PEs from the harassment meted out by the plethora of Government agencies. It has also advocated for bringing the salaries and incentives in PEs on par with those prevailing in private sector enterprises, and has urged the Government to grant autonomy in price fixation to PEs. It has suggested induction of professional members on the board and elected members to represent those who hold the disinvested shares and the non-Government shareholding. It has cautioned the Government that enough care should be taken to ensure that new incumbent is put in place sufficiently in advance of the retirement of the existing incumbent at the top level of PEs. It has also suggested that the Government should select strategic investors and operationalise recommendations of the Rangarajan Committee excepting in the case of strategic PEs. It is of the opinion that the shareholdings of the Government could be brought down to the extent of 26%, to keep with the Government the power only of blocking the special resolutions. It has suggested that as a general principle, wherever appropriate, PE should be restructured for disinvestment in order to ensure enterprise value. The Commission has also suggested the extension of safety net to the workers affected by the disinvestment exercise. Though the Commission has been in existence for more than two years, it is not clear about its identity. The Department of Industry, in February 1997, dipped the wings of the Commission further by taking away its power to appoint global consultants. Only some of the recommendations of the Commission have been accepted. On many recommendations, the Government has not taken any action. Peeved by the Government's indifference, one of the members quit the Commission and the others have exhorted to continue. The Government's indifference has make a mockery of the Commission.

Critical Analysis

A critical analysis of the disinvestment exercise points to a lack of clarity about the goals of disinvestment. Disinvestment programmes of the Governments of the UK, Singapore and Malaysia have been comprehensive in nature and have accomplished both the short-run and the long-run signposts. These programmes have had tremendous impact on the growth of capital markets.

In the Indian case, some public enterprises were bunched together for disinvestment. The portfolio of enterprises selected for disinvestment does not lend itself to any logical explanation. In Singapore, there was a consensus to disinvest shareholdings in all PEs. Canada and Spain started disinvestment in loss-making PEs. The UK and Chile followed exactly opposite approach. PE disinvestment in India represents a mixed bag of enterprises.

In Mexico, Romania and Russia, small PEs have been preferred for disinvestment. In Canada, UK and Pakistan, core PEs have been chosen for disinvestment. Pakistan, Poland and many other east European countries have gone for full disinvestment, rejecting partial disinvestment. Of course in the case of the Polish PEs, restructuring was attempted before privatisation. The policy-makers in India have exhibited their ignorance about the merits of partial versus full disinvestment. In India, the Government has gone for partial disinvestment. Of course, there have been cases of full disinvestment in the case of some state-level PEs. The success, has also been partial. The success of partial privatisation in India is plagued by the presence of Article 12 of the Indian Constitution, the CAG (Comptroller & Auditor General) audit, and the fear of vigilance. Even the Navaratna initiative falls short of the desired expectations as the freedom to recruit, sell, produce, and enter joint ventures remains a myth.

The process of disinvestment is full of shortcomings. In the UK, initial price offers were make to get the feel of the right price. In France, the fixed price method was used to disinvest the shareholdings. Again, in France, UK, and Malaysia, the stock market route was employed to off load the shareholdings. The Indian disinvestment programme also suffers from lack of involvement of PE executives and excessive domination of the bureaucrats. The speed and control are the other two aspects crippling the forward movement of the disinvestment programme. With an investment of Rs. 1,93,000 crore, the disinvestment realisations fund about Rs. 11,300 crore, which measure up to a mere 5% of the total investment (a mere 1% per annum). This realisation turned out to be about 39% of the overall target of Rs. 29,000 crore for disinvestment between 1991-92 and 1997-98. On the other hand, fresh investment in PEs turned out to be four times the disinvested amount during the period 1991-97.

In the UK, France, Chile, Singapore and Malaysia, the rate of disinvestments was very high because of the introduction of the "Golden Share" concept which is akin to the "veto" power exercised by the permanent members of the UN Security Council.

The disinvestments have been resorted to without developing a relevant database, which was criticised by the CAG.

In France the valuation is done by two independent banks, and the figures are reviewed by the Privatisation Commission. The final price recommended to the Government by the Privatisation Commission could in no instance be reduced by the Government.

The policy-makers have given no regard to the capital market dimension of the disinvestments. In the case of countries, such as the UK, France, Malaysia and Singapore, capital markets have been reformed by the introduction of measures such as dematerialisation of shareholdings, removal of restrictions on the repatriation of payment of dividend and interest, listing on stock exchanges and foreign bourses, etc. In India, some of the disinvested PEs have even applied to the Securities & Exchange Board of India (SEBI) to exempt them from submitting the quarterly returns (Indian Petrochemicals Corporation Limited being one such enterprise). There are other enterprises queuing up to do this. The status of the machinery of disinvestment is a significant factor affecting the efficacy of the disinvestment programme. In France, a separate Privatisation Commission has been set up to deal with disinvestments. In Malaysia and Singapore, separate bodies have been set up under independent Acts to carry out the disinvestment programme. In Mexico, a unit of seven people in the Ministry of Finance reports directly to the top of the political hierarchy on disinvestments. In the case of Philippines, a separate Asset Privatisation Trust has been formed with a qualified businessman as its head. In Malawi, the Department of Statutory Bodies, a single institution under the Government, handles disinvestment. In Kenya, a decentralised structure with different holding institutions were made responsible for disinvesting the elements in its portfolio.

Any well-devised disinvestment programme would always show a high concern to the welfare consequences of the disinvestments to workers, consumers, Government, and buyers. In case of the UK's National Freight Corporation, Mexico's Telmex, and Chile's Enersis, workers were involved in the disinvestment exercise. To thwart any loss to consumers, regulatory bodies were set up in UK, France, China and Mexico. In India, a small advance in this direction has been made by setting up the Telecom Regulatory Authority of India and the Insurance Regulatory Authority. These have not made the desired mark, have locked horns with the Government, and remain almost non-starters. Most of the enterprises in the UK, Chile, Singapore, France and Argentina undertook internal and external restructuring in order to make disinvestment an interesting proposition. The elements of commercialisation, corporatisation, and privatisation were injected very deep in the bodies corporate. In South Africa, in order to prevent the culture of non-payment, users councils were set up. Even systems like ISO-9000, ISO-14000 benchmarking and a statement on the performance of the board of directors in a given period, were introduced in the UK, South Africa and New Zealand. Financial restructuring was done in case of several enterprises in the UK by carrying out appropriate adjustment in the debt-equity mix and infusion of equity by private parties. Product policy changes were carried out to strengthen product-mix, market share, quality, R & D, etc. Labour restructuring was undertaken to adjust the labour force. In case of the UK, the Parliament exercised the right of self-denial to questions on PEs. In the case of French PEs, the Government shareholdings have been deliberately brought below 50% by a system of interlocking of shareholdings, in which some major financial institutions have each a stake of 2-5% in the shareholdings. This way, they obviated the need for an extensive control of the Government while ensuring broad control of the Government on these enterprises. In India, the picture regarding the internal and external restructuring has been dismal. Interest of labour has not been protected as introduction of the provision of safety net has been ignored. The National Renewal Fund has been put forward only to bay a lip service, the State Renewal Funds set up by the Government of Rajasthan and a few other State Governments have been cosmetic in nature.

New Framework

Disinvestment in PEs are the need of the hour. This would serve the twin purpose of making PEs competitive, and finding funds for restructuring in addition to meeting a part of the fiscal deficit. However, the Government has not proceeded the right way in initiating disinvestments. Its strategy for disinvestments has been flawed on a number of counts. It is, therefore, necessary to evolve a new framework to effect disinvestment, which may include the following elements in its design:

Restructuring

Instead of identifying some enterprises as candidates for disinvestment right away, it would be more appropriate to restructure PEs which have not been functioning as per the desired benchmarks. This restructuring may include several aspects such as legal, financial, and physical, and improving the environmental interface with the interacting agencies, most prominent of which are committees of the Government and also its various organs. This would allow the Government to maximise the receipt of revenues from disinvestments and also enhance acceptability of disinvestments for the buyer in the private sector.

Corporate Governance

A closely associated problem with restructuring is concerned with corporate governance. State of the art of corporate governance would mean introduction of effective internal management systems at the enterprise-level, owning up responsibility for achieving results at the board-level, and practicing the right of self-denial at the Government-level. This would also mean a tacit understanding of the fact that, other things remaining the same, there is no difference in public and private enterprises.

Government Shareholdings

The good and bad attributes in an enterprise are also linked to shareholdings owned by the various parties. In India, the Government enjoys the monopoly shareholdings in PEs. The Companies Act, under Section 619, defines a company as a Government company when the Central Government or the State Government, or both the Central and the State Governments together, own 51% and more shareholdings of the company. Nowhere in the world, any Companies Act defines a Government company in this manner. Though the Krishnamurthy Panel suggested retention of 51% of shares by the Government in strategic and core enterprises and the Rangarajan Committee approved this by and large, it would be in the fitness of things to bring this down to 26% to give the Government the right to have its say in blocking resolutions of special importance. Prominent business houses such as Birlas and Tatas, and several other business groups, have shareholdings of the same order. The international experiences gained by Singapore and Korea reveal that a new concept of Government ownership has already come into practice. This entails Government-linked undertakings, in which the Government has reduced its shareholdings to the levels 5-25%, with a Golden Share at its disposal. The reduction of shareholdings would free the enterprises from the constraining provisions of the Indian Constitution, and the limitations imposed by the Government ownership in the form of multiple audits and vigilance controls. They would also be free from following, the Government rules in regard to purchase, recruitment, etc. which work to their disadvantage. They could have their own salary structure which would be competitive with respect to that existing in the private sector.

Capital Market

The development of the capital market should precede before any disinvestments. Here, the definition of capital market may include in its ambit even the international capital market which may allow PEs to have access to the GDR route and external commercial borrowings. PEs selected for disinvestment may look to book-building, creation of special purpose vehicle, and direct placements.

Legal Requirements

Recently there was a writ petition filed by Prof. Bob Mathew in the High Court of Karnataka, arguing for discontinuance of the disinvestment exercise by the Government of India. The writ petition questioned the right of the Government to disinvest without taking into confidence the labour, and also its decision to allocate a part of the disinvested shareholdings to the workers and managers under Article 253 of the Indian Constitution. The honourable court, after taking various legal and judicial aspects into consideration, moved that it was within the domain of the Government to undertake disinvestments, and that it was competent to part with the shareholdings to the workers and managers. However, the essence of the story is that it would be appropriate for the Government to discuss these issues with various stakeholders, and also foresee problems which may create hurdles in the path of disinvestment. The Government would do well to have a holistic look at the existing laws and the international practices in this regard.

Database

The creation of a database is an essential condition for disinvestments. Such a database should cover information about the industry and its functioning in India and abroad. It should also contain various possible valuations for a company which is proposed to be taken up for disinvestment. The Disinvestment Commission recently observed that it would like to urge upon the Government to provide facilities to it for creating a database and recruiting experts. It is difficult to understand as to how the Commission could function without such experts on it, and without the setting up of such database, for a period of two years, and submit a number of reports in which specific schemes have been suggested for certain PEs.

Disinvestment Commission

The Commission's working has run into rough weather. Instead of making it an independent body, its wings were cut by making it an executive body. As noted earlier, the Ministry for Industry, further clipped its wings by taking away its powers to appoint global consultants and advisers. A separate Act must be brought about which lays down what should be the affairs of the Commission and its mode of functioning. The French experience of the Privatisation Commission has been appreciated world-wide. The French Privatisation Commission has gained a respectable stature and has become a non-political organisation, whose advice is taken as final in matters regarding disinvestment and privatisation.

Involvement of PEs

It is necessary to involve the officials of the PEs which are proposed to be disinvested by the Government. In UK, the Government carried out disinvestment exercise in consultation with the concerned PEs. British Gas and British Telecom were not exceptions to this practice. Even in France, once the Government lists out the names of PEs for disinvestment, the rest of the exercise is left to the French Privatisation Commission and the concerned enterprises. Such an exercise would enable the valuers/consultants to assess the value of the enterprise based on the replacement cost method.

Regulation

It would be appropriate first to put in place the regulatory agencies before taking up important enterprises for disinvestment. The petroleum enterprises would require the setting up of a regulatory authority before disinvestments therein. Similarly, the infrastructural enterprises would require a regulatory authority. In the case of the disinvestments in British enterprises, the office of the Telecom Regulatory Authority was set up before the privatisation of British Telecom, and similarly the regulatory authority for the power sector was set up before privatising the energy enterprises.

Welfare Consequences

Care should be taken to prevent loss to consumers, workers and other stakeholders resulting from disinvestments. We have already suggested creation of a comprehensive safety network for workers.

Conclusion

The disinvestment exercise initiated in 1991 could not progress smoothly due to a number of limitations resulting from the Government's shortsightedness and lack of vision. The bureaucratic meddling also hampered its smooth execution. The research studies show that disinvestments have not resulted in an improvement of the performance of the disinvested PEs. This is because no steps have been taken to bring about changes in the internal management of these enterprises and restructure the Government-enterprise interface. The creation of the Disinvestment Commission in 1996 has been of no consequence as it has remained a non-starter, and most of its recommendations have not been taken cognisance of by the Government. Disinvestment is of much importance today as the Government can bring through this policy instrument both a change in the operating style of these enterprises and also raise funds to mitigate its fiscal deficits. It is here that the international experience can be very useful to the Government in making its disinvestment process effective and result oriented. The Government would do well to have a separate enactment to set up a Privatisation Commission on the model of the French Privatisation Commission. The Government under such a law should specify the enterprises to be disinvested, and the Commission set up under such law could then effect disinvestments in consultation with the concerned PEs. The Government should improve the corporate governance, create competitive capital market conditions, and carry out the necessary legal reforms. It should also bring down its shareholdings considerably to 26% to overcome the problems created by Article 12 of the Indian Constitution, CAG and audit, and the interference of vigilance. Further, restructuring of PEs should precede any disinvestment exercise. The brief overview of experience of disinvestment in India, together with an international comparison clearly brings out the fact that the Indian exercise has proceeded haphazardly and that much remains to be done in terms of restructuring, legal reforms and taking care of mechanisms to cope with adverse impact on certain stakeholders.

Table 1
Contribution of Disinvestment Proceeds Twoards Bridging the Fiscal Defict

Year	*Total amount raised (Rs. crore)*	*Fiscal deficit as % of GDP*	*Contribution of disinvestment towards bridging fiscal deficit*
1991-92	3038.000	5.89	0.49
1992-93	1912.510	5.69	0.27
1993-94	2290.986	7.52	0.29
1994-95	2619.620	6.10	0.28
1995-96	198.620	5.90	0.02
1996-97	390.00	[illegible].2	0.01
1997-98	940.00	6.1	0.01

Source: Krishna Yamuna, Disinvestment – The Indian Way, IPE Journal, Vol. 3 & 4, July-December, 1996, pp. 166-169.

3

Disinvestments–How to Go About it?

—R.K. Mishra

As a part of the new economic policy, the Government of India initiated disinvestments in public enterprises in October, 1992. Seven years hence, the Government has mobilised Rs. 18,288 crore (41.28%) against the cumulative target of Rs. 44,300 crore from 39 enterprises. The Government has mobilised Rs. 1479 crore till November, 1999 as against the target of Rs. 10,000 crore during the current year. The NDA Government proposes to employ disinvestments in public sector as a strategic tool to restructure the national finances in order to revitalise the Indian economy. It essential at this juncture to assess the disinvestment experience of 1998-99 to draw suitable lessons to place the disinvestment exercise on the fast track for 1999-2000.

In 1998-99, the different heads of the Government spoke in different voices showing that there was hardly any coordination in their thinking displaying their utter disregard to the fact that they were organs of the same body. They embarrassed themselves often by making contradictory statements. Their casual approach gave a world-wide impression of the lack of professionalism and will to learn from the global experiences. The policy makers exhibited their inability to see the big picture of the problem as they reflected the limitation to their intellect to see the problem at the best in some parts which probably could best sub serve the interest of their client groups.

It was argued that the formation of the trust would rid public enterprises of the Government Control and provide an ease of action to sell the shareholdings transferred to fill back the Government coffers.

The Government officials in the best traditions of the civil service saw the impending danger of losing control on public enterprises and using them as whipping boys. The Finance Secretary to the Government of India, hard pressed to mitigate the fiscal deficit, introduced a new concept.

The special purpose vehicle as per the Finance Secretary's views, was the best way to put disinvestment programme on the fast track and achieve the initial target of Rs. 5,000 crore set for the year 1998-99. According to this concept, a special purpose vehicle (SPV) with a limited capital investment (it is said that there are 30,000 SPVs with an average capital of Rs. 10,000 each) was to be set up to which the share capital of the enterprises to be disinvested was to be transferred. The SPV in return would approach the financial institutions/capital markets to pay back the money to the Government against the equities off loaded by the Government. Another concept suggested was that of the 'warehousing' which meant sale of shares to the financial institutions for the purposes of realisation of equity values and keeping such shares in bank vaults as long as they could not realise the best value. The Unit Trust of India (UTI), the biggest mutual fund as also the biggest buyer of public sector shares, stung by its failure of efficiently managing US 1964, was not ready to accept the generous invitation of the Government lest it crumbled and to take the last breath. The other financial institutions sensing the ultimate danger joined the UTI and refused to tiptoe the Government. The failure of the disinvestment programme of the highly financially successful enterprise, Container Corporation of India Limited (CONCOR), which had earlier pitched the sale of shares at Rs. 450 per share and had to climb down later to agree to a price of Rs. 225-230 per share shook the other entreprises which were to disinvest their shareholdings including the Oil and Natural Gas Company Limited (ONGC) and the Indian Petro Chemicals Limited. The financial institutions seeing virtue in the CONCOR shareholdings picked up the disinvested stake only to realise that the shares of trading in the range of Rs. 210-180 undermining their capitalisation. The Government had fixed a target of realising Rs. 5000 crore from disinvestment in 1998-99 which was revised later to Rs. 9000 crore. The Government realised Rs. 6190 crore as on March 31, 1999. The bulk of this amount of Rs. 6190 crore was realised through the controversial cross holdings. Having succeeded in this, the Finance Minister set a target of Rs. 10,000 crore for disinvestments for 1999-2000. The IOC, GAIL, MRL, MTNL, VSNL, HZL and ITDC shareholdings are slated to be on block in 1999-2000.

The increasing fiscal deficits, left no choice for the policy-makers and the Finance Minister and the Finance Secretary but to have a greater reliance on disinvestments of the shareholdings of the public enterprises. This led to the innovations of 'buy back of shares' which implied acquisition of the Government shareholdings by the cash rich enterprises. This obviously worked in the favour of the Government but turned out to be a huge dent in the cash flow of the disinvested enterprises affecting the tempo of their investments in R&D, expansion and maintenance. This also worked at cross purposes with the Government's new economic policy initiative of making public enterprises gain in terms of size and operations. To net more proceeds from this process, the Finance Ministry suggested the public sector oil enterprises to give effect to cross shareholdings in their equities which could benefit the Government on the one hand and the public sector oil enterprises on the other by enhancing coordination and integration of upstream and downstream operations and may also offer the advantage of economies of scale. Some common directors on the Board of such companies were introduced apparently to defend the concept. However, only the future will tell as to whether the so-called advantages materialise or not. Nonetheless, the Government has succeeded in making public enterprises worse off by the cross holding investments as it has realised the money arising out of such transactions. The oil companies in the public sector picked up for the cross holdings instead of becoming global giants are faced with cash crunch explaining in more than one word about the lack of justification for this method of disinvestment employed by the Government. The IOC-ONGC swap hit price hitch with both companies settling for a pricing following which the stock prices fell by at least fifteen to twenty per cent:

The erstwhile Disinvestment Commission went ahead with its work. It submitted twelve reports during its tenure covering 58 enterprises. The Commission's recommendations in general did not find favour with the Government. The chairman of the Commission and some of its members threatened to quit the Commission. The Commission did not make any impact as it continued to be an executive body manned both at the top and at the administrative level by bureaucrats. Its members though eminent had not significant interface with disinvestments earlier. The Commission did not develop any database in the absence of which its recommendations missed the requisite research back up. The Government dilly-dallied the appointment of its members and extension of tenure. It will be in the fitness of things that the process of disinvestment should be left to the concerned enterprises which could carefully examine the matters such as readying themselves for disinvestments, preparing their own calendars for disinvestment exercise, timing and pricing of shareholdings and extent of their disinvestment. The valuation of shares is a complex problem. The pricing of the shares of GAIL as a part of the current year's disinvestment programme has been widely questioned. Further, the Government has not been able to adequately explain the logic of the valuation as per the replacement cost method which it proposes to follow henceforth. There is need to build appropriate capacity in this area within the country. A total dependence on foreign consultants is not in the national interests.

If disinvestments have to be used as a technique of restructuring of public enterprises, the time is ripe for the Government to give a fresh look towards its objectives of disinvestment. The financing of fiscal deficit should be relegated to much lower place in order as compared to upgradation of technology and provision of safety net as the objectives of disinvestment. Sadly, all that Government has done in the realm of disinvestments has been nothing more than implementing the programme only in letter and missing in its spirit cent-per cent. Hardly any consideration has been given to readying public enterprises for disinvestments. In a nutshell the programme has jumped straight from a naught to nine without caring for the intervening steps. The process of introducing user charges, commercialisation and corporatisation has been thrown to wind. The results are for any one to see. The share prices of the listed public enterprises over a period of one year show a steep decline in the case of Steel Authority of India Limited, Bharat Earth Movers Limited, Indian Petro Chemicals Limited, Indian Telephone Industries, Balmer Lawrie Limited and its associate Balmer Lawrie-Van Leer to mention a few. The market has taken note of the government's unwillingness to withdraw from public enterprise and remove the sinister shadow of civil servants and discounted any hope for future as the Government and its civil service have discredited practically every important move to reform.

To conclude, if disinvestments have to contribute to the success of the economic reforms, it is necessary that the policy makes adopt positive methods of divesting public sector shareholdings instead of the passive methods employed during 1998-99. Such an approach will promote competitiveness, development of domestic capital market, globalisation of public enterprises, strengthening of internal organisations and systems and superior post privatisation efficiency.

4

Multiple Agencies: A Bottleneck for Disinvestment

—R.K.Mishra & B.Navin

Since the very beginning in July 1991 the Government have considered the various issues concerning machinery for disinvestment for the Central Public Enterprises (CPEs). Initially the task rested fully with the Department of Public Enterprises (DPEs) whose recommendations were weighted by the Cabinet committee on economic affairs only to be finally cleared by the Cabinet. The implementation of the recommendations remained with the DPE, GOI. Later on to facilitate mature decisions an empowered committee of secretaries was setup to process the recommendations regarding disinvestment by the DPE. To give impetus to the disinvestment programme, the Government setup a disinvestment commission in 1996. Although during 1991, the Government planned to set up an independent agency to oversee the process of disinvestment, finally the disinvestment commission was established under an executive order having the reporting relationship to the Minister for Industries. The commission faced rough weather when its power to appoint foreign consultants were taken away by the Ministry and further its wings were clipped by marking its role purely advisory. This is reinforced by the fact that of the many recommendations made by the commission, the recommendations accepted by the Government do not even cross single-digit . Even the commission's recommendation of the presentation of the reports to the Cabinet was cold shouldered. The Government in early December, 1999 constituted a dedicated department for disinvestment headed by Shri Arun Jaitely, Minister of State for

Information & Broadcasting. The department will deal with all matters relating to disinvestment, including the modalities for sale, restructuring, pricing and other issues related to the sale of Government equity. The CPEs would however continue to report to their parent Ministries for all other purposes. It is argued that such distancing is necessary to ensure that parent Ministries do not scuttle the disinvestment process for fear of losing control and power. The Government is also proposing to reconstitute an advisory disinvestment commission as the last commission lapsed on November 30, 1999.

A peep into the various changes that have been effected with regard to the disinvestment machinery clearly brings out the fact that it is cumbersome, multi-layered and non-conducive for a speedy implementation of the disinvesment targets. Though the creation of separate department weakens the resistance offered by other Ministries, it does not provide any safeguard against the bureaucratic dilly-dallying and non-adherence of the calendar detailing the various activities for disinvestment. The creation of the department is superior to the DPE but it falls drastically short of an autonomous agency accountable to the Parliament. Moreover, the continuation of the disinvestment commission in the erstwhile form is likely to cause the recurrence of the tug of war which existed between the erstwhile commission and the Ministry for Industries.

The multiplicity of agencies has been identified as a negative factor arresting the smooth functioning of the disinvestment process. This is why in most of the countries opting for disinvestment, a full-fledged autonomous agency has been created accountable to a body none other than Parliament. In Australia, a State owned industrial company, Organisation for the disposal of Industrial Assets of the Government is responsible for the privatisation of industrial assets. In France, the Commission for privatisation, established under the Privatisation Law (1982), looks after the disinvestments of the Government enterprise. In Italy, the privatisation committee has been set up to effect disinvestments. In Poland, the Ministry of Privatisaion in consultation with the other Polish Ministries undertakes disinvestment. In South Africa, the Ministry of Public

Enterprises is in charge of disinvestment. In Jamaica, a privatisation team is responsible for disinvestments of public enterprises. In Mexico, the privatisation unit takes administrative responsibility for selling public enterprises. The unit supervises the sales while the details of the sale are delegated to the agent banks. In Sri Lanka, the Private Enterprise Reform Commission (PERC) oversees the entire privatisation process. The Ministry of Capitalisation in Bolivia has the exclusive mandate of implementing the privatisation/ capitalisation policy of the Government. The Divestiture Implementation Committee (DIC) in Ghana is responsible for the divestiture programme and reports to the Committee of Secretaries. In Albania, the National Agency for Privatisation (NAP), a Government agency accountable by law to the Council of Ministers is responsible of the disinvestment. In Venezuela, Venezuela Investment Fund acts as the holding company for all the PSEs. The president of this fund is also the chairman of the privatisation commission. In Peru, the implementation of the disinvestment programme rests with the Committee for Implementation (CEPRI). The Privatisation Board is the implementing agency in Pakistan. In Jordan, the Executive Privatisation Board (EPB) acts as the implementing agency. The policy decisions are arrived at the level of Higher Ministerial Council (HMC) headed by the Deputy Prime Minister which are delegated to the EPB. In Tunisia, the policy decisions taken by the Commission for Restructuring of Public Enterprises (CAREP) are passed on to the Director General of Public Enterprises for implementation.

If the international experience in disinvestment is any guide, it is clear that in India we will have to take privatisation and disinvestment as interchangeable terms. This ensures the success of the disinvestment programme in that it does not preclude restructuring, mergers, formation of sectoral companies and trade sales. In Sri Lanka the process of disinvestment has been christened as *peoplisation*, in Chile as *de-nationalisation*, in Australia as *privatisation*, in Brazil as industrial transition, in Costa Rica as *economic democratisation*, in Egypt as *partners in development*, in Tunisia as *restructuring*, in New Zealand as *assets sales programme* and in Mexico as *dis-incorporation.* It is thus clear that if the newly created department on disinvestments has to be a success, it must hasten to confer the autonomy to the proposed new disinvestment commission and could act as a go-by between the commission and the Cabinet assuming among other things, the role of processing the recommendations, but certainly not undermining its authority and independent functioning. As an alternative to the present machinery it may be worthwhile consider transferring the entire disinvestment programme and the task of its implementation to the Planning Commission which is involved in resource mobilisation and their allocation. The Planning Commission also possesses the required expertise in terns of competent advisers and have the understanding of the time element. As a coordinating body, it has effective access to the Ministries and Government departments. The deputy chairman, Planning Commission, is a special invitee to the Cabinet who obtained a good understanding of the Indian Financial System in his stint as chairman of the Tenth Finance Commission. In anyway, association of Planning Commission is vital to inject a fresh vigour to the disinvestment programme.

The Government in its statement on December 16, 1999 assuring the appointment of a new disinvestment panel observed that disinvestment should be shaped by four basic factors viz, best public interests, maximum value, transparency in process and utmost protection of workers' interests. This impinges upon the newly created department on disinvestment to build proper infrastructure support in terms of an indepth understanding of the business of each CPE, valuation of its shares as per different methods, linkage of public enterprise with capital markets and private sector potentialities. The department cannot any more commit costly mistakes of being unprepared whenever presentations are made in international bourses. The proposed disinvestment commission on its part cannot afford to imitate its predecessor which was largely inward looking. Though it published its reports, and had initially about of a few seminars, its methodology was questionable and resultantly the recommendations failed to make a dent.

5

Memorandum of Understanding in India: A Backdrop

P. Geeta

The public sector, which was synonymous with public good in most countries, is currently being viewed from a newer perspective. The public enterprises in India during the post Independence era were brought into existence as instruments of social good. They are now viewed as having become overextended and a drain on the nation's economy. As these enterprises are also unable to make profits, which was not a strong motivation when they were set up, the Government of India, already over burdened with other development responsibilities has lately realized that the public enterprises are a responsibility which it cannot fulfil. In the present era of liberalization and privatisation there is a widely shared opinion that the public enterprises cannot be considered as organizations seeking only non-commercial purposes. So the performance of public enterprises is being assessed on par with organizations that are engaged purely in commercial activity.

There has been a continuous effort on the part of the Government of India to build up opinion regarding the need to make the public undertakings more '*self managed enterprises*' than thrive as parasites on public exchequer. The role of government is being redefined to exclude the micro economic decision-making from its agenda. A wave of reforms has swept the developed countries, countries in transition and developing countries alike. In transitional economies, privatisation is the centerpiece of national economic transformation. The reform and privatisation of public enterprises and development of the private sector are central strategies to their development plans.

PUBLIC ENTERPRISES IN INDIA: AN OVERVIEW

Basic Philosophy and Ethos

The Public Sector in India was an initiative by the policy-makers after the attainment of India's Independence in 1947. The basic philosophy and ethos of Public Sector highlighted the need for creating a comprehensive network of infrastructure facilities to promote speedy industrialization and rapid economic development in the country. At the same time it was the aim of the policy-makers to make available all essential services to public. The philosophy stressed the need for rectifying regional imbalances and promoting balanced regional development throughout the country. A significant feature of the basic philosophy and ethos of public sector in India was to take up these developmental activities irrespective of the risk involved namely heavy investment, low returns, and long gestation periods. The need of the hour was that the public enterprises should take up the initiative of providing social justice through equal employment opportunity to all. The intention was not to make profits out of these enterprises, though they were not started with an intention to incur losses either. The aim was to generate resources through public sector for financing other developmental programmes initiated by the Government.

Objectives

In order to appreciate the role of the public sector, it might be necessary to recapitulate the state of economy at the time of India's Independence in 1947, and the problems confronting the country which needed to be tackled in a planned and systematic manner. Thus, State's interaction in all the sectors of the economy was inevitable, because private sector had neither the necessary resources nor the managerial skill, nor the will to undertake such risks. In the view of the nature and variety of problems faced by the country in its economic, social and strategic fronts, it was a pragmatic compulsion to deploy the public sector enterprises as instruments of equitable economic growth.

Thus, it can be said that public sector enterprises are recognizably distinct organizations of the government, whether Central (union level) or State (provincial level) or local (municipal level), involved in production, distribution or any other services, economic or social in nature. Taken as a whole they cover a very broad range of activities in accordance with the factor of affordability of people and the essentiality of the service.

Diversification of Public Sector

Public sector has played a pivotal role in the planned economic and industrial development of the country. For the purpose of planning and national accounting, public sector in India includes all activities funded by the government. Thus, the size of the public sector is indeed very large, as shown in Tables 5.1 and 5.2. It includes not only the government departments but also the government companies, whether in the Central or State sector, irrigation and power projects, railways, posts and telegraphs, ordnance factories and other departmental undertakings and banking, insurance, financial, and other services.

Table 5.1 : Growth of India's Central Public Enterprises

Sl. No.	*Year*	*No. of Enterprises*
01	1951	5
02	1956	21
03	1961	47
04	1966	73
05	1974	122
06	1980	179
07	1985	215
08	1990	241
09	1995	245
10	1996	244
11	1997	242
12	1998	240

Source: Annual Public Enterprise Survey, Department of Public Enterprises, GOI, New Delhi.

Table 5.2 : Activity Composition of Public Sector

Activity Enterprises	*Central Public*
Production of Goods	
Minerals & Metals	22
Energy including Coal & Petroleum	27
Chemicals & Fertilizers	29
Engineering & Transport	51
Consumer & Agor-based Industries	37
Total	**166**
Rendering Services	
Trading & Marketing	18
Consultancy & Development	12
Transport & Communication	13
Financial Services	7
Contracting & Construction	10
Tourism & Ohters	15
Total	**75**
Under Construction	4
Grand Total	**245**

Source: Annual Public Enterprise Survey, Department of Public Enterprises, GOI, New Delhi.

Government's Industrial Policy on Public Sector

The Industrial Policy enunciated by the Government of India from time to time highlighted the critical role of the public sector in the country's economy and accordingly the Government provided the necessary policy and financial support for its growth.

In the 1948 Industrial Policy Resolution, the industries were divided into three broad categories viz (i) relating to defence (ii) new undertakings to be started by the Central, State and Municipal Corporations which were given exclusive powers for starting them (iii) the category which included the sectors of iron and steel, coal, ship building manufacture of telephones and wireless.

The 1956 resolution was the guiding factor, which gave a strategic role to public enterprises which started expanding from core areas to non-core areas. The State Owned Enterprises (SOEs) were given opportunity to take new initiatives in this respect Private efforts were also invited to supplement the efforts. Thus taken as a whole, the Government of India has been providing continuous support and encouragement for the development and diversification of public sector units.

Thus, the Industrial Policy Resolutions of 1948 and 1956 laid the foundation for the public sector in India and allowed it to grow to the position of *commanding heights* of the economy; as envisaged by Nehru, the first Prime Minister of India, by reserving all strategic industries under the purview of Government. The establishment and expansion of all core sectors, basic, strategic and infrastructure industries were made the responsibility of the Government. The increasing investment and encouragement provided by the Government to these vital sectors, resulted in building up high hopes on their performance. However, for a variety of reasons, their performance has not been commensurate with the investment made and encouragement provided by the Government from time to time. The Bureau of Public Enterprises Survey Part-I highlights this fact. Gradually the process of performance evaluation started assuming importance.

The Janata Government in 1977 envisaged that the public enterprises were an instrument for socializing the means of production. In 1980, the Government inspite of its faith in the public sector, did not allocate any resources for its expansion.

On 24th July 1991 the Government of India as a part of the 'Statement on Industrial Policy' announced a 'Statement on Public Sector Policy' also[1]. It aimed at improving the portfolio and performance of public sector. The statement contains the following decisions:

(1) Portfolio of public sector investments will be reviewed in order to focus the public sector on strategic, high-tech and essential infrastructure. Although some reservations for the public sector

was being retained, there would be no bar for areas of exclusivity to be opened up to the private sector selectively. Similarly, the public sector will also be allowed entry in areas not reserved for it.

(2) Public enterprises which are chronically sick and which are unlikely to be turned around will for the formulation of revival or rehabilitation scheme be referred to the Board for Industrial and Financial Restructuring (BIFR), or other similar high level institutions created for the purpose. A social security mechanism is being created to protect the interest of workers likely to be affected by such rehabilitation packages.

(3) In order to nurse resources and encourage public participation, a part of the Government's share holding in the public sector would be offered to mutual funds, financial institutions, general public and workers.

(4) Boards of public sector companies would be made more professional and given greater powers. The system of Government administrative sanctions has now been replaced by conferring the operational and managerial autonomy to the management of the enterprise concerned with a view to secure better results.

(5) There will be greater thrust on autonomy through MOU systems through which managers would be granted greater autonomy and will be held accountable. Technical expertise on the part of the Government would be upgraded to make the MOU negotiations and implementation more effective.

(6) To facilitate a fuller discussion on performance, the MOU signed between Government and the public enterprise would be placed in parliament. While focussing on major managerial issues, this would also help place matters of day to day administration of public enterprises in their correct perspective.

Public Sector Performance — a brief overview

Since 1991, the country has opted for the policy of liberalization, and has gone ahead with Structural Adjustment Programme (SAP) and policy changes to being in market discipline as part of the economic reform process. This has necessitated the Government to open up the sectors hitherto reserved for public sector both for domestic and global competition. In this transitional economy, during the recent years of economic reforms with increasing measures of liberalization, several public enterprises have shown improved performance in terms of production and productivity as also financial profitability. However the loss incurring public enterprises are losing more and these include the public sector enterprises where the Government stopped the budgetary support.

Despite the fact that the Government also initiated partial disinvestment programme since the year 1991-92, it has not been able to realize the expected amount out of the divestiture. India as a transitional economy intends to distance the government from the commercial enterprises. But it is unable to take hard options of complete privatisation in areas and sectors even where private sector initiatives can meet the market demands. India, like any other developing society is unable to relinquish its interest in public sector. This situation has therefore, resulted in a seeming dilemma on the part of the Government that if the public sector must continue, it must justify its existence in the competitive environment.

Concern with regard to MoU Signatory Enterprises

The MOU signatory enterprises have steadily grown from 4 enterprises signing the MOU in the year 1987-88 to 109 enterprises in 1997-98. *Annexure-I* gives the list of the enterprises signing MOU in the year 1997-98. *Annexure-II* gives the ratings of enterprises signing MOU between 1990-91 and 97-98. It shows that in a period of seven years the percentage of 'excellent' public sector enterprises varied between 24% and 54%. While the aggregate pattern remained the same, there were substantial variations in terms of individual public sector enterprises. For example, of those evaluated, 51% were rated 'excellent' in 1990-91, which came down to 28% in 1992-93. The percentage went up to 41% again in 1993-94 only to show a downward tend of 39% in 1994-95. In the year 1995-96 it was 30% and again it came down to 24% in the year 1997-98 as shown in *Annexure-III.* But the fact remains that the demarcation of ratings between 'very good' and 'excellent' could be due to marginal variance in points.

There is another way to look at the enterprises, which have signed the MOU, whether their financial performance has been commensurate with their MOU performance. This does not seem to be the case with enterprises like ONGC that was rated 'excellent' in 1993-94 but its profits came down by Rs. 30 crore form the previous year. In contrast, the case of petroleum sector when analyzed shows that all the nine public sector enterprises in the petroleum sector has signed the MOU have shown an increase of 19% in gross margin and percentage of capital employed to turnover went up from 173% in 1993-94 to 223% in 1994-95. This was mainly due to the upward revisions in the administered prices. This is a fact that we tend to overlook that there has been an additional infusion of investment amounting to Rs. 1422 crore during the year 1994-95 alone in the sector. But the public sector enterprises in the petroleum sector have not been rated as 'excellent'. Thus the five-point scale on which the performance of the enterprise is evaluated may not always reflect the real performance of the enterprise.

In view of the uncertain performance there has been a growing concern for the public enterprises, which has brought about the initiation of a number of policy measured by the Government. The decision on disinvestment in public sector has been a significant step taken by the Government in this respect, in the early 90's.

Disinvestment and MOU

In the decade much effort has gone into privatisation by sale of public enterprises to private sector. Though disinvestment is a new process and difficult as well, it has become attractive to the Governments, which are faced by financial demands in maintaining their public enterprises. The largest and the least profitable enterprises cause the biggest deficits. And these are the ones that are most difficult to privatise. The experience of the countries with policy of divestiture has been that they have found it difficult to manage the excess labour in public enterprises, valuation of public enterprises, lack of regulatory framework after privatization, shortage in capital for purchasing the enterprises under sale etc. All these problems have been the reasons for the policy on divestiture not being able to achieve the expected results. In the case of India 50 Central Public Undertakings (CPU's) were slotted for divestment but the government could do away with only 40 of them till 1997-98.

An assessment of the relationship of divestiture with the MOU system at this point is essential. Divestiture calls for selling the enterprise away to a private party while the system of MOU talks about regulation and performance of the enterprise within the established framework of the government. Table 5.3 gives the list of enterprises and the disinvestment figures along with the Government holding. All the enterprises listed below are essentially MOU signatory enterprises.

Table 5.3 : Disinvestment in the MOU Signing Enterprises

Name of the Enterprise	*Total Disinvestment(%)*	*Govt. Holding(%)*
ONGC	3.86	96.14
IOC	8.74	91.14
VSNL	33.04	66.96
GAIL	3.40	96.60
BHEL	32.28	67.72
HPCL	48.94	51.06
BPCL	33.80	66.20

Source: BPE Survey, 1997-98, GOI, New Delhi.

The impact of the policy of divestiture on the MOU signatory enterprises needs to be analyzed against this backdrop. The fact remains that disinvestment in these enterprises has in no way lessened the Government holding of 51% of the share of the capital. Thus the enterprises though subjected to disinvestment are still under the Government holding and subjected to all the necessary regulations. The system of MOU under these conditions seems to be affected minimally, as these enterprises are still regulated by the Government and are a part of the evaluation process.

Policy Measures for Making Public Sectors Efficient

MOU was adopted in 1985 in response to the widely held perception that the public sector enterprises were less efficient due to lack of operational freedom. The other strong reason that supported the introduction of the MOU system was that the public enterprises were unable to perform as they were pulled in different directions by a number of agencies which were responsible for the enterprise functioning under the ministry concerned as an overall supervisor. For example, Finance Ministry controlling the budget, the Planning Commission regulating the project appraisal and the aid-givers like the IMF, World Bank and others influencing the policy decisions. These organizations set conflicting objectives for the enterprises, and pull them in different directions. This leaves the enterprises with a very little scope to take decisions both (financial and managerial) which can improve their performance.

The system of MOU has been in vogue for more than a decade. It seems to have a marginal impact on the public enterprise performance. It has not been able to provide autonomy to the enterprises, both financial and managerial, which was one of the major objectives for the introduction of the system. The issue of autonomy has still not been set in place and the issue of accountability still remains dicey.

The Navratna Package

In the wake of the factors, the Government on the 4th of July' 97 flagged off the NAVRATNA package. It selected nine PSU's financially and managerially empower them to emerge as "*Global Giants*". The unshackled blue chips are BHEL, HPCL, IOC, NTPC, IPCL, SAIL, VSNL, and BPCL. This package provides them with certain powers to these enterprises keeping the necessary control over them[2].

(1) Incur all capital expenditure without any monetary ceiling.

(2) Enter onto technology joint ventures and to obtain, by purchase or other arrangements, technology and know-how.

(3) Raise debt from the domestic capital markets and to borrow from the international capital market.

(4) Effect organizational restructuring, including establishments of profit centres, opening offices in India and abroad.

(5) To structure and implement schemes relating to personnel and HRM, or even compulsory retirement schemes.

At another level, these units will be able to set up joint ventures and wholly owned subsidies in India and abroad. However, the equity limits to Rs. 200 crore on any project, which can be raised up to Rs. 1000 crore depending on the nature of the project undertaken. Thus the concept of Navratna gives considerable scope for autonomy.

The introduction of this package will certainly have an impact on the performance of the PSU's. They will have more freedom to take decisions in financial and managerial matters, which will have a direct impact on their performance. The lacuna caused by the MOU system has been filled up by the introduction of the Navratna package.

The Mini-Ratna Package

In pursuance of the policy objective to make the public sector more efficient and competitive, the Government decided to grant enhanced autonomy and delegated powers to the profit making public enterprises, subject to eligibility criteria and guidelines provided by the Government. The Government categorized the enterprises into the following[3];

(1) *Category I PSE's* : PSE's should have made profit in the last three years continuously, the pre-tax profit should have been Rs. 30 crore or more in at least one of the three years and should have a positive net-worth.

(2) *Category II PSE's* : These PSE's should have made profit for the last three years continuously and should have a positive net-worth.

For enhancing financial and operational autonomy for the profit making enterprises and for improving their efficiency a number of measures have been brought out by the package:

(1) Restructuring of the Boards of the eligible enterprises for improving financial and operational autonomy, by including three non-official directors to making it more efficient.

(2) Capital expenditure up to 300 Rs. crore to be spent by the enterprises for purchase of equipment etc.

(3) Joint ventures up to Rs. 100 crore to be taken up by the enterprises without permission from the Government.

(4) Structure and implement schemes relating to personnel and human resource management, training, voluntary retirement schemes, etc.

The package has enhanced the scope for improving the financial and operational autonomy for the enterprises and has certainly provided the necessary boost to the enterprises to plan their projects and ventures as per the situation. It has facilitated the enterprises to take concrete decisions in matters of human resources and R&D and other related issues, which will boost the performance of the enterprise and will lead them to success.

Problems and Issues of Public Sector

The Government and the public enterprises have a very close and complex relationship. The Government is the majority shareholder and it has to ensure that the policies for the public enterprises are compatible with the national objectives and priorities. The relationship between the public enterprise and the Government is affected by a number of factors, a few of them have been listed below[4]:

(i) *Prior Approval:* On a number of matters such as expenditure, joint ventures, creation of new posts, reappointment. Decisions can be taken only after the prior approval of the Government.

(ii) *Directives:* The Government has power to issue directives for matters which it considers sufficiently important and for which there is no provision of control or otherwise.

(iii) *Circulars and Office Orders:* These cover a whole range of operative matters, and though informal in nature are generally adhered to by the public enterprise.

(iv) *Board Appointments:* The Government appoints the Board of Directors.

(v) *Reports, Returns and Meetings:* The Ministries and Departments receive numerous reports and returns, and review meetings are held.

(vi) *Power of Supervision:* In a few cases the Government can supersede a statutory corporation.

(vii) *Power of Investigation:* Through the Central Bureau of Investigation and the Vigilance, the government controls the public enterprises.

Performance Evaluation in Public Enterprises: Problems & Issues

As a prelude to understanding public enterprise problems it is essential to appreciate its environment, which has far reaching effects the functioning of the public enterprise working. The public enterprise environment is a complex phenomenon and needs to be conceptualized. The reasons for this are many, the most essential one being the changing socio-political conditions in the country, which have a direct effect on the performance of the public enterprises. Productivity and profitability of Indian public enterprises has been adversely affected by a variety of factors. Some of the prominent among them include,

(a) Too much of interference by the members of the political and administrative elite in the working of enterprises.

(b) Domination of bureaucrats on the Governing Board of public sector units and in the decision-making process.

(c) Absence of sound policies, in different functional areas of management.

(d) Excessive government controls, and lack of operational and managerial autonomy.

(e) Problems of time and cost overruns due to enormous delays in the execution of assignments.

(f) Lack of concern for quality and inability to meet customer's expectations.

(g) Poor profitability and low returns on investments.

(h) Too much of government protection to public sectors, and lack of dynamism on the part of the managements concerned.

(i) Excessive growth control, and regulation and lack of delegation and decentralization of powers.

(k) Decision-making through approvals, sanctions and ratifications in all the functional areas of management.

(l) Poor and excessive inventories and under-utilization of installed capacity.

As a result of the above problems and handicaps, the public sector management's have not been able to give a satisfactory account of their performance over the years. Further, the Government could not evolve satisfactory criteria for performance evaluation. This was largely due to lack of clarity of objectives for public enterprises.

The Government Structure

The environment of public enterprises has at the top the President of India, and all the powers of the majority shareholders vest with him. The Cabinet is the final arbiter in all the matters of policy issues like floating a new government company, expenditure beyond laid down limits, and schemes of grouping or regrouping of public enterprises. The Minister and the Administrative Ministry concerned have a critical and most frequent interaction with the public enterprises at both formal and informal levels.

Another important constituent is the Planning Commission. Its project appraisal division and various sectoral divisions play an important role in the clearance of capital projects. The Finance Ministry, which is the most powerful ministry, has to be approached for providing necessary financial clearances. The Home Ministry concerns itself with the vigilance through the Central Vigilance Commissioner and the Central Bureau of Investigation (CBI). The Labour Ministry regulates employment policies, provides general guidance on industrial relations and informally interferes with the cases of industrial disputes.

Foreign collaborators and aid givers like the IMF, WB etc. have their own influence on the organisation. The Members of Parliament (MPs) as well as the Members of Legislative Assembly (MLAs) have their own reasons for interfering in the working of the enterprises. Parliament is perhaps the most important constituent of the public enterprise environment. The Committee on Public Undertakings (CPOU) has direct and substantial interaction with the public enterprises. The Comptroller and Auditor General's (CAG's) influence on the public enterprises is substantial and regular.

Statement of Problem

The public sector was set up in the post-Independence era as an instrument for the development of Indian economy. The Industrial Policy Resolutions of 1948 and 1956 gave the public enterprises necessary stimulus to develop both in their number and investment. The resolutions covered every conceivable field ranging from steel to petroleum, fertilizers, and basic drugs, chemicals and aeronautics where India was considered to be lagging behind the advanced countries.

After a certain period of time the policy makers realized that the public sector had reached the stage of "commanding heights" only in size but has failed to give the expected results in all other fronts. In order to rectify this mistake a number of countries went in for privatization, though the phenomenon of privatisation has not worked the way it should have. This was the time when the policy-makers around the world realised that there had to be an intermediate step between privatization and government ownership. This possibility was explored in the performance improvement[5]. While we do not have a formal institutionalized evaluation system, the performance of public enterprises is in fact being assessed in a number of ways.

Firstly, there is the Annual Public Enterprise Survey, brought out by the Bureau of Public Enterprises which also identifies the top ten profit-making and top ten loss-making enterprises. This document largely influences the perceptions of general public in regard to public enterprises. The Planning Commission in the context of the formulation of the five-year plans as well as the annual plans makes another broad appraisal of the performance of public enterprises. There have also been appraisals and reviews of certain public enterprises by the Comptroller and Auditor General of India. There are several Parliamentary committees, which undertake investigations of the activities of public enterprise and produce reports on them.

The Economic Administrative Reforms Commission known as the (Jha Commission) went into the issue of evaluation of the performance of public enterprises in 1984. The commission suggested that for each public enterprise there should be a document setting for the basic expectations of the Government in arriving at the relevant investment decisions, and that with reference to that primary governmental charter, each of the public enterprises should attempt a corporate statement of goals and objectives[6].

This was followed by the setting up of the Arjun Sengupta Committee in 1985, which dealt with the issue of improving the performance of the central public enterprises and recommended for setting up of a performance contractual system. The contractual system was named as the "*Memorandum of Understanding*". The MOU's have been in operation in Indian public enterprises since 1987, commencing in an experimental way with four public enterprises. The number of public enterprises, which signed the MOUs, has gone up to 109 in the year 1997-98. The system has remained so far confined to the central public enterprises and has not percolated to the state level public enterprises. *Annexure-IV* gives the number of CPE's entering MOU between 1988-98.

The main goal of the MOU system as articulated by the government was to reduce the '*quantity of control*' and increase the '*quality of accountability*' by specifying in explicit terms the measurable goals and giving the enterprise operational autonomy to pursue them. It is an annually negotiated document between the administrative ministry concerned and the top management of the public enterprises. This exercise is carried out in the presence of the Ad-hoc Task Force (ATF) comprising of experts, civil servants (retired), and former Chief Managing Directors. This is done with a view to introducing neutrality and objectivity to the process.

The MOU includes the following format:

(a) Corporate mission	Long-term objectives
(b) Objectives	
(c) Performance criteria	Short-term objectives
(d) Targets (quantitative and qualitative)	
(e) Weightages assigned to the criteria	
(f) Obligations of public enterprises	Obligations
(g) Obligations of the government	
(h) Speical privileges of MOU Signing managements	Special Privileges

Over the years the weightages have been increasing in favour of financial performance and now it stands at 60% comprising of gross margin and net profit. Now further addition of ratio of net profit to net worth is marked as an important financial indicator. The rating for MOU signing enterprises varies on a 5 point scale for ranging from 'Excellent', 'Very good', 'Good', 'Fair' and 'Poor' based on the annual assessment of the performance on the given criteria.

The overall basic purpose of introducing the concept of 'performance contracting' in the form of MOU in India is to improve the performance of the public enterprises by giving the required and timely support from the Government as well as operational autonomy. But still there is very high degree of demand from public enterprises for infusing professionalism in the management, autonomy and distancing of government form the public enterprises.

Objectives of the Study

(1) To highlight the background in which the performance contracting was introduced in India and giving a detailed account of the system in India and in the global context.

(2) To study the mechanism of performance contracting in Indian Public Enterprises and giving an overview if the global context.

(3) To highlight the process of performance contracting in India, including the target setting evaluation etc and comparing it with other countries.

(4) An appraisal of the system of Memorandum of Understanding (MOU) in Indian enterprises with the help of a questionnaire survey and taking up individual case studies.

(5) Suggesting measures for improvement in the current MOU system.

Research Design

The Universe

The study covers the broad spectrum of MOU's in India with particular reference to select public enterprises. Appropriate references are made regarding the performance contracting in other countries like Korea, Pakistan, Ghana, Gambia, Sri Lanka and China. This has helped in conceptualizing the framework for the study and drawing suitable conclusions.

The Sample

The study concentrates on the experiences from select Central Public Sector enterprises. These enterprises are dealt with comprehensively and the performance of these enterprises before signing the MOU and after signing MOU is examined. At the same time an overview of the experiences of all the 109 Central Public Sector enterprises signing the MOU is projected in the study. A questionnaire schedule is used as a tool to project the experiences of all these 109 enterprises to get a holistic view of the working MOU system in India. The responses obtained from these enterprises are included in the study to substantiate the theoretical exercise with the practical experiences. Individual cases of two PSU's signing MOU for more than 8-10 years is done in order to give an in-depth analysis of the system of MOU in India.

Research Methodology

The study adopted a careful methodological approach. Induction method was followed for this study. In order to propagate the logic support, the theory by case studies, and to highlight the empirical method. Theory and facts are brought together in such way that an empirical trend can be traced in the study.

Tools and Techniques

Since the study calls for facts, various methods of data collection have been employed. The details of the tools of research for collection of data include:

(1) Collection of all available literature from the library, newspapers and other sources.

(2) Consulting records from the Department of Public Enterprises as well as the public enterprises themselves for data on the MOU.

(3) Collection of information from the key persons involved in the MOU process.

(4) A questionnaire is prepared for collecting data from the MOU signing enterprises.

Sources of Data

The following constituted the sources of information for the purpose of the study:

(1) Balance sheets of the Public Enterprises.

(2) Bureau of Public Enterprises reports

(3) Database for the Bureau of Public Enterprises

(4) Center for Monitoring of Indian Economy reports.

(5) World Bank Publications.

(6) Economic and Political Weekly

(7) IPE Journal

(8) Economic Times

(9) Financial Express.

(10) Parliamentary Publications

(11) Comptroller & Auditor General reports.

(12) Other relevant research work and publications of scholars related to the area of study.

(13) Books and publications related to MOU.

(14) Collection of information through questionnaire schedules.

(15) Individual discussion with the PEs and the BPE officials.

Survey of Literature

The survey of literature on MOU has been classified under the following heads.

On Public Enterprise Philosophy and Policy Issues

Public enterprises in India and abroad have been studied extensively as shown in the survey of literature. But the vital issue of performance evaluation--basic philosophy, mechanism, tools, and techniques employed deserve to be examined from qualitative angle.

Y. Raghavaiah examines the role of public enterprises in the third world countries in his paper[7]. He noted that the origin and growth of the public enterprises in the third world are conditioned by a completely different set of forces and circumstances in contrast to those in Western experience. While the public enterprise in the West reflect the dynamics of social and economic reality, this is not so in developing countries. The author is of the opinion that the philosophy of the public enterprise in developing countries is different from that of those in the developed countries. The expansion of public sector in the developing countries has mainly emphasized the development administration.

Nitish De[8] discusses the vital problem of organizational analysis in public enterprises and suggests various approaches to organizational analysis. The author has studied five public sector organizations and one private sector firm. He concludes that, (i) The higher the age, the more the energy generating activities (ii) The higher the position, the grater the authority and more discretionary the contents of the job. (iii) The shorter the length of the service, the greater is the energy draining activity and (iv) Energy cost is higher in work activities within the department/division/function.

B. L. Maheshwari,[9] draws attention towards the managerial effectiveness in the public enterprises in India and says that it is at its lowest ebb in the public enterprises. He observes that action has to be taken from the side of the managers of the public enterprises and the government also should be working on creating a positive atmosphere. There is a problem of low pay package to the employees and lack of recognition at the managerial levels of the enterprise. All these factors indicate a need for toning up the performance of public enterprises.

Geeta Gouri[10] in her paper argues that most of the collaborations with the transnational corporations have been technical in nature. An overview of the case studies presented by the author indicates that the public enterprises and the Government of India have not utilized their bargaining powers to the fullest extent.

On Autonomy and Control

T. L, Sankar,[11] examines the extent, scope and necessity of executive controls, with special reference to the Indian case. He holds the view that the relative weights of social responsibility in the overall objectives of public enterprise influences the degree of autonomy and accountability. In the units that are purely commercial in nature there is more autonomy for they are provided with detailed guidelines spelling out the role of the government executives and that of the professional managers. In such undertakings there is a greater possibility to determine objectives clearly and prioritize them. The author emphasizes a need for greater understanding between the public enterprise as well as the government so that the conflicts are resolved amicably.

Jagadish Prasad[12] discusses the dilemma of maximum control, which is desired by the parliament and public, and the maximum autonomy desired by the public enterprise management. Accountability according to the author has been organized through two channels, the ministerial as well as from the parliament. The author is of the opinion that the public enterprise should not be under the control of the minister for day to day operations, though it should be broadly accountable on policy matters. The author suggests the need for a healthy practice in the area of legislative provisions and conventions.

Om Prakash[13] emphasizes the need for objectivity in evaluating the performance of public enterprises on the basis of given objectives. He observes that the vagueness in objectives would be a major constraint on the judicious evaluation of the public undertaking performance. He proposes a qualitative and quantitative evaluation to ensure a balance between the autonomy and accountability of the public enterprises.

On Management Development and Training

Udai Parekh[14] discusses the practices of human resource development in the public enterprises. After examining the distinctive features of public enterprise management, he feels that only a systematic management of human resources will help public enterprises achieve the objectives for which they have been set up. The most important features that need to be taken care of are the management of rewards.

Shiva Ramu[15] is of the opinion that manpower planning in public enterprises has been a neglected function. He deplores the prevalence of unhealthy practices in the appraisal of public enterprise personnel. He believes that the training systems need to be toned up to develop competent individuals to accomplish organizational goals.

On Performance Contracting Philosophy

Ramanadhan[16] focuses on the basic purpose of a performance contract in the case of a public enterprise. It has by design, not gone into the many important aspects of implementing it, which are usually considered, important. The author highlights the point that the performance contract must spring from a consideration of its basic purpose, or else it operates on loose foundations. The autonomy with which the managers operate in the circumstances of their markets makes the full success of a performance contract. This depends again on the nature of publicness of a given public enterprise. The performance contract helps the parliament and the public in visualizing the rationale of a public enterprise, its operating efficiency, and the government's own role in its management. Thus, it helps in drawing up detailed provisions of the contract, specially relating to the responsibilities of the government under the contract.

Y. Venugopal Reddy[17] discusses the highlighting features of Memorandum of Understanding in India. He discusses how the MOU formalizes the relationship between ministry and the public enterprises. By signing the MOU greater transparency is expected. The author refers to the performance contracting in France. The experiences with Performance contracting in France were dissatisfactory, though contractual system cannot be totally refuted it has certainly initiated thought process in the enterprises regarding their own objectives of policy and the instruments of execution.

K. R. S. Murthy[18] Evaluates the effectiveness of the MOU system introduced in the India public sector enterprise after considering the recommendations of Sengupta Committee Report, 1985.

This edition by Kidwai and Sahai,[19] has seasoned managers heading huge public sector enterprises, candidly discuss their experiences in running their industries. The difficulties faced by the industry in interacting with some of the ancient laws of the land on one hand, and ensuring smooth labour relations on the other have been amply explained.

The papers deal with areas of socio-economic environment, organizational problems, and management issues, upgradation of technology and international experiences are discussed.

Prajapathi Trivedi,[20] surveys the theoretical basis and country experiences of the French system of contracts as a technique to rationalize government controls of public enterprise's in order to improve their performance. Starting with the theoretical foundations of the system, the paper describes its nature, history and practice in France and makes a critical analysis of the theoretical justifications for its design and listing a set of preconditions for its successful implementations. The experiences in less developed countries (LDC's) with the use of the French model or variations thereof are surveyed. These include Senegal, Gambia, Pakistan, Korea, Bangladesh and India. The paper concludes with summary of lessons or conditions for successful implementation of the contractual approach. They include political commitment at the highest level as well as throughout various levels of government and emphasize the importance of training.

R. K. Mishra[21] reiterates the importance of public enterprises in the planned economic development in India. It is therefore, vital that the public sector enterprises accelerate the socio-economic growth. The paper deals with how educational and training programmes for the public enterprise board members, executives and removal of external barriers, may be used as tools to secure a better performance evaluation for the public enterprises in the future.

Victor Powell[22] discusses about the public enterprise systems in developing countries. It has a concern about the operations of these systems and the constraints of the environment in which the public enterprises have to operate. It discusses about various dimensions of performance and operating effectiveness and how they can be measured. By 'effectiveness' is implied to the enterprise objectives and the extent to which these are achieved. Since public enterprises in developing countries seldom have clearly defined, unambiguous and consistent objectives, the attempts to assess their effectiveness are frequently met with frustration.

Emphasis is given on the need for the public enterprise to add wealth to the community, and to help raise the standard of living and undertake investment, which will generalize opportunities for, improved consumption. It also emphasizes the need for improving planning, control at the enterprise level and develop action plan for performance improvement of the enterprise.

This paper is based on Shreedhar Sharma's[23] thesis on state Financial Corporation submitted for University of Paris. Here, the author discusses the nature of the public enterprises, being enterprises they are expected to perform specific functions and at the same time unlike their counterparts in the private sector they are supposed to subserve the 'public interest'. The evolution of the contractual system is traced in the annals of the French public enterprises. The objectives with which the contracts originated are discussed which are essentially improving their financial situation, fixing investment of these enterprises over a given period of time and at the same time fixation of productivity norms. The author also discusses the advantages of contractual system for the betterment of public enterprises; i.e., by codifying relationships between government and enterprise by target setting, specifying nature of government aid. At the enterprise level the advantages of performance contracting is manifold, it helps in strategic planning, greater sense of satisfaction to personnel introduces a sense of commercial functioning in the enterprise introduces Management by Objectives (MBO) and enhances autonomy.

On Country Specific Experiences

Mohnot[24] talks about the concept of performance contracting, as to why was the need felt for a contract and how it originated as an effective instrument for improving the performance of public enterprises. The contents of a contract are discussed that it should thrust to accountability, generate more autonomy, and contain targets to be measured in a fixed span.

The Indian model of performance contracting (MOU), is discussed at length. The government claim as per the authors reference to a DPE Survey that MOU System has now stabilized. The public sector enterprises signing MOU's have achieved the targets fixed by the Finance Ministry and the Planning Commission, the MOU Policy seems to have been successful as per a report given by the Government of India, DPE, Public enterprises surveys.

Prajapathi Trivedi[25] in this paper essentially deals with the experience of the Korean enterprises with the signalling system and makes a comparison of the signalling system with MOU system adopted in India. The paper descriptively gives the public sector scenario in Korea and how the GIE's were initiated into the performance contracting with the Act of 1984. It also highlights the post contract scene in Korea. The differences and similarities between the Indian MOU system as well as the Korean system are discussed at length.

T. L. Sankar[26] systematically analyses the MOU system in India. He has brought out the hard facts about the MOU system and has highlighted the total set up of the system right from the institutional arrangements, contents and implementation.

Trivedi[27] highlights through this article, highlights the changes which MOU policy underwent relating to (i) format (ii) institutional arrangements for drafting and monitoring MOU (iii) differences relating to process and procedures involved.

Trivedi brings an overview of the complete institutional structure for the MOU Policy. The various organs for designing MOU's as well as for implementing them are discussed at length. The author justifies the present set up for the MOU.

Mary Shirley[28] provides an assessment of Pakistan's performance evaluation system for its Industrial Public Enterprise (IPE's). The paper gives a brief history and description of the system. It calculates the impact of the system on performance and management of enterprises. The paper concludes with recommendations to adopt the system in other countries. The assessment is carried out to: (i) provide suggestions on way to strengthen the system (ii) inform officials of other countries interested in replicating the system (iii) suggests ways to adopt it in other countries.

Ramaswamy Iyer[29] discusses the experiences of India with Performance Evaluation Systems in relation to public enterprises. The past experiences and efforts are highlighted in the Central Public Sector Enterprises.

Shahrokh, Roya[30] prepared a census of the contract plan experience in Africa. Issues on the contract plans expansion across Africa, and the industries using them are explored. Fact finding objectives in individual country reports highlighting the known facts and the lesson learned in the process does an assessment of the contract plans. The positive and negative points of the contract plan and a list of recommendations for the future users is given. Alternative mechanisms for controlling public enterprises are also brought out.

Ninety-six instances of contract plans in the public utility sector were explored. The various lessons learned by them are highlighted and a need is expressed to find an alternative to the signalling system as a better mechanism for controlling the public enterprises.

Ravi Ramamurthy[31] in this paper, compares the programme contract used in the France and Senegal and the signalling system, which is used in Pakistan and South Korea is discussed at length.

Prajapathi Trivedi[32] discusses about the evaluation system for the public enterprises. He is of the view that though the public enterprises must be evaluated like the private enterprises, they should not be evaluated on the basis of same criteria as the private enterprises.

Ramamurthi[33] discusses the main features of the Korean system of performance evaluation for public enterprises. The various aspects are discussed like the technical aspects of the Korean System, which comprises of target setting, giving weightages and values ending up with an evaluation and reward. The organizational aspects like the structures of the contractual system and staffing is also mentioned. The second part deals with some observations on the system citing the examples of Korean Telecom Authority discussing how the performance criteria and weightages are decided upon and how the evaluation begins and ends with a reward or punishment.

Song, Dae-Lee[34] essentially highlights the economic development of Korea during the last 30 years, and the role of public sector played in the economy. The paper reassesses the importance of the Korean public enterprise sector and the impact of the new

Korean public enterprise policy. The policy for the Government Invested Enterprise in 1984, brought in the contractual system for the 25 industries (GIE's). An assessment is made at the end as to how the policy has worked and its impact on the Korean economy is also highlighted. The utility of the Korean system of performance evaluation to other developing countries is discussed at the end.

Leroy Jones[35] gives due importance to the Korean effort for improving their public sector enterprise performance. Though Korea has developed the world's most sophisticated system for evaluating performance of its public enterprise the implementation of the system has been done in such a way that the enterprise behavior has actually changed as a result. The author attacks the indicator categorization, i.e., qualitative *Vs* quantitative, results Vs processes, non-duplicative Vs duplicative indicators. The problems existing with criteria value determination, criteria selection is also highlighted. The problem of duplication is dealt with in details. The need is also highlighted for improving qualitative, indicators by focussing on marginal changes, staffing etc.

Ramamurthy[36] briefly reviews the fundamental problems governments' face in controlling the public enterprises. The report recommends an innovative approach to the strategic planning and control of non-financial public enterprises (PE's) in Bangladesh. The report offers the performance contracting system as a possible solution. Further, it describes the units of applying the performance contracting system or an experimental basis to two public enterprises (NBPM GENCO).

Park Young[37] reviews role of the GIE's in Korea, which is represented by far the most important category of public corporations. It traces the unsatisfactory performance of the Government-Invested Enterprises, leading to the promulgation of the Government Investment Enterprise Management Act, which introduced extensive institutional and legal reforms. The paper then goes on to describe the various characteristic features of the system and reviews the results of the evaluation conducted for its first two operational years, 1983 and 1984. Finally, the paper assesses the system's performance and attempts to draw some conclusions that will be useful for other countries, which may consider adopting a similar system.

Leroy Jones[38] argues about the need for improving the efficiency of the public enterprise sector. A basic indicator of efficiency is first derived and then modified to account for some of the exogenous factors beyond the control of management. Given a criterion, which is broadly applicable across enterprises, it is necessary to establish criteria values deviating 'good' from 'bad' performance. The next step would be to allow for non-commercial objectives and growth for dynamic effects. The need in fact is to implement the performance evaluation method in a phased manner for enterprises. Finally, the feasibility of proposed methodology is examined by its application to one Pakistani public enterprise.

Istaqbal Mehdi[39] deals with the most important aspect of contracting system i.e., target setting. Setting targets for operating units is an exercise of reviewing the annual operational plan of enterprises, identification of cost inefficiency areas and a negotiated agreement to improve performance by way of agreeing to a set of targets for the enterprise management. Negotiation and establishment of acceptable and achievable targets reflecting good performance is a challenge both to the management of an enterprise as well as to evaluating agency (EAC), Experts Advisory Cell. The exercise of target negotiation provides an occasion to identify weak areas in the enterprise operations. This paper attempts to illustrate Pakistan's efforts to improve cost efficiency in public enterprises by way of target setting for evaluating performance. The first section deals with the concept of target setting, the second with performance evaluation exercise in Pakistan's context, the third section highlights the process of target setting in the context of Pakistan.

Shaikh Hafeez[40] provides an overview of the public enterprise sector in Pakistan. It traces how the contracting system originally developed in Pakistan's enterprises and also highlights how the system was actually implemented by the government of Pakistan. It explains the deviations from the system, actually proposed and the system implemented. The paper includes with an assessment of the success of the contracting system in Pakistan's public enterprise performance improvement.

On Performance Contracting for State Owned Enterprises

Sankar, Nanndagopal, Mishra,[41] discuss at length the background for working of State Level Public Enterprises (SOEs) and a need to take initiatives to improve their performance. The need for the introduction of MOU system in the (SOEs) is felt as a necessary prerequisite for their proper functioning.

Venon Raymond[42] says that in relation with their SOEs governments try to capture the advantages that are thought to exist in operating through autonomous organizations. At the same time, they attempt to push the enterprises towards a set of governmental goals. The interface between ministries and managers of SOE's has to be considerably different from those of the private enterprises. Thus governments are attempting to improve the relationship with their SOEs through contracts. This step cannot be ruled out as a significant one.

Mallon Richard[43] deals with the performance contracts between government and SOE's to regulate the hierarchical exchange of reciprocal commitments. The simplest form of contracts is mentioned as the single period contracts, the multiple period contracts prove expensive. Performance contracting is not a panacea for improving the performance of SOE's, instead they should be viewed as a step towards creating self correcting organizations.

This paper is a commentary by Beesely, M.E., Likierneas, A, Bloomfield[44] dealing with United Kingdom, France and Italy. It reflects the levels of dissatisfaction with the performance of government enterprise. The issues addressed are relating to accountability, efficiency, policy direction etc. There are common to all the countries in Europe.

Menon, Krishna, Umapathy, Srinivasa[45] discuss that there is no unique control system that is suitable for all SOEs that is appropriate to all types of organisations. The type of control system needed is a function of certain organisational objectives and the measurability of organisational outputs. This paper classifies SOE's into four groups on the basis of their features and suggests improvements for the design of organizational control system.

Shirley, Mary[46] discusses the characteristics of the programme contracts in France. It deals with how the programme contracts originated in France. The experience of contracting with some of the SOE's in France for providing full management autonomy to the companies, which were nationalized in 1982-83. The results of the improvement in some SOE's, through with loosening of government controls.

Shirley, Mary[47] discusses Senegalese government negotiated controls with 5 SOE's since 1980. This paper studies the experience of the contracts and points out the fact that SOE's were forced to do strategic planning for preparing the contracts and simultaneously made the government systematically compare their cost of social objectives and investment proposals with their benefits.

On United Nation Publications

There are some valuable publications by the United Nations regarding performance contracting for public enterprise.

The book entitled Performance Contracting for Public Enterprises[48] deals with each country experiences with contracting system giving a complete picture of the economy's policy of the country and the need felt for the system.

Another publication Guidelines for Performance Contracting[49] deals with how performance contracting is dealt with the different countries. It gives a guideline for preparing performance contracts with country specific needs.

A World Bank Policy Research Report,[50] discusses the various aspects of reform in the state owned enterprises. The contracting system for the SOE's have been studied in detail and an evaluation is made of their success functionally. It deals with specifically the dynamic factors like the political will and economic factors in a country, which help in shaping the policies for reform.

Another book on Performance contract[51] deals with the concept and rationale of performance contracting in public enterprises, the institutional arrangements needed for designing and implementing the contracts, as well as the monitoring and evaluation procedures involved in it, country experiences of specific enterprises are also included in the publication.

Gaps in Literature

The performance contracting system in the global context has received great attention in the academic circles. There are a few gaps in the literature that has been identified during the course of the study. Firstly most of the writings are of the time when the system was hardly introduced in the public enterprises. After a system is introduced it takes at least 5 to 6 years for the system to become operational and highlight results. Secondly, all the literature that has been available only focuses about the `quantitative' target setting and their evaluation. There are very few articles, which highlight the `qualitative' aspects of an enterprise, which are equally important. This study is conducted keeping these gaps in view and an attempt is made to reduce, if not fill these gaps through this study.

Notes

1. Annual Public Enterprise Survey, Department of Public Enterprises, GOI, New Delhi, 1996-97, p. 3.
2. Report published by the Economic Times, July, 1997.
3. *Op cit.*
4. Laxmi, Narain, *Principles of Public Enterprise Management*, S. Chand & Company, New Delhi, p. 20.
5. Iyer, R. *Past Experiences with Performance Contracting in India: Lessons from MOU.* Paper presented at an MOU workshop organised by BPE & IIM Calcutta. New Delhi, 1989.
6. *Op.cit.*
7. Raghavaiah, Y., *Public Enterprises in the Third World Countries – An Emerging Scene*, in edited Vol. of Sankar, T.L., Mishra, R.K. & Ravishankar, S. "Leading Issues in Public Enterprise Management", Himalaya Publication, Bombay, 1985, p. 8.

8. De, R. Nitish "*Organizational Energy – A Diagnostic Exercise*", in Sankar, T.L., Mishra, R.K. & Ravishankar, S. (ed.) "Leading Issues in Public Enterprise Management", Himalaya Publications, Bombay, 1985, p. 15.

9. Mahaeshwari, B.L. "*Managerial Effectiveness in Public Enterprises*", in Sankar, T.L. R.K. Mishra, & Ravishankar, S. (ed.)" Leading Issues in Public Enterprise Management", Himalaya Publication, Bombay, 1985. p. 20.

10. Geeta Gouri, "*Transnational Corporations and Public Enterprises in India*", in Sankar, T.L., Mishra, R.K. & Ravishankar, S.(ed.) "Leading Issues in Public Enterprise Management", Himalaya Publication, Bombay, 1985. p. 25.

11. Sankar, T.L. "*The Government Executive and the Public Enterprise: A Study of The Supervisory Control System*" in Sankar, T.L., Mishra, R.K. & Ravishankar, S. (ed.) "Leading Issues in Public Enterprise Management", Himalaya Publication, Bombay, 1985, p. 30.

12. Prasad Jagadish, "Autonomy and Accountability of Public Enterprise – *Facts and Issues*" in Sankar, T.L., Mishra, R.K. & Ravishankar, S.(ed.) *"Leading Issues in Public Enterprise Management,* Himalaya Publications, Bombay, 1985, p. 50.

13. Prakash Om, "*Public Sector Performance Evaluation*", in edited Vol. of Sankar, T.L., Mishra, R.K. & Ravishankar, S. "Leading Issues in Public Enterprise Management", Himalaya Publication, Bombay, 1985, p. 55.

14. Parekh Udai, "*Human Resource Development in Public Enterprises*", in (ed.) Vol. of Sankar, T.L., Mishra, R.K. & Ravishankar, S. "Leading Issues in Public Enterprise Management", Himalaya Publication, Bombay, 1985, p. 42.

15. Ramu Shiva, "*Improving Public Enterprise Performance Through Appraisal, Training and Management Development*", in (ed.) Vol. of Sankar, T.L., Mishra, R.K. & Ravishankar, S. "Leading Issues in Public Enterprise Management", Himalaya Publications, Bombay, 1985, p. 48.

16. Ramanadhan, V.V., "The Basic Purpose of a Performance Contract", Paper presented *at International Conference on Performance Contracting*, New Delhi, 13-15, January, 1997.

17. Reddy, Y, Venugopal *Public Enterprise Reform and Privatisation,* Himalaya Publishing House. Bombay. 1992.

18. Murthy, K, R, S. "More Memorandum less Understanding", *Economic and Political Weekly,* 26 th May 1990.

19. Kidwai, Waris, K & Sahai, Baldeo, "Dynamics of Management of Public Enterprises, "Edited by. *SCOPE,* New Delhi. 1989.

20. Trivedi; Prajapathi. "Theory And Practice of Contractual Approach: Lessons from Lower Developed Countries with Performance Contracting", *Journal of International Center for Public Enterprises,* Vol. 8, No.1, 1988, Lubjyana, Yugoslavia.

21. Mishra, R. K. "Performance Evaluation of Public Enterprises in India", *Institute of Public Enterprises Journal,* Secunderabad, 1988, Volume XI, No. 4, Page No. 1.

22. Powell Victor "Improving Public Enterprise Performance (Concepts and Techniques)", *Management Development Series* No. 22, International Labor Office, Geneva, 1982.

23. Sharma Sreedhar "The Enterprise Contract System in Public Enterprise Management", *Institute of Public Enterprise Journal,* December 1982. Hyderabad.

24. Mahnot, S R. "Basic Issues in Performance Contracting Systems with Special Reference to Indian Case", Paper presented at the *International Conference on Performance Contracting,* New Delhi, 14-15th January 1997.

25. Trivedi Prajapathi and Suresh Kumar "Memorandum of Understanding and The Korean Performance Evaluation System", *Institute of Public Enterprise Journal,* Volume 13, No. 2, 1990, Page No. 567.

26. Sankar, T. L. "Memorandum of Understanding; The Wrong End of the Stick", *Journal of Public Enterprise,* Volume 13, No. 2, 1990, pp. 72 to 78.

27. Trivedi, Prajapathi, "Methodological Issues Relating to Recent Changes in the MOU Policy", *Quarterly Journal of AIMA,* Vol. 29, No. 7, July 19, 1990.

28. Trivedi, Prajapathi, "Institutional Arrangements for Designing and Implementing Memorandum of Understanding", *Management in Government Journal* , New Delhi, 1990.

29. Shirely, Mary. M. "Public Enterprise Performance Evaluation System in Pakistan", *World Bank Discussion Paper*, 1988.

30. Iyer, Ramaswamy R "Past Experiences with Public Performance Evaluation System in India: Lessons for MOU's", paper presented at *International Workshop on MoU's organized by Bureau of Public Enterprise and Indian Institute of Management,* Calcutta, March 6-9th 1989, New Delhi.

31. Shahrokh, Royal Jone" The Contract Plan Experience in Africa", Paper submitted for partial fulfilment of MBA, Graduate School of Business Administration, University of California, Berkeley, December, 1987.

32. Ramamurthi, Ravi "Methods for Controlling Public Enterprises: International Comparators", Report submitted to the *Ministry of Finance Government of Bangladesh and the United Nations,* April 1986.

33. Trivedi, Prajapathi "Public Enterprises in India: If Not for Profit Then for What", *Economic and Political Weekly,* Volume XXI, No. 48, November 29, 1986.

34. Rammurthi Ravi "Observations on the South Korean System for Performance Evaluation of Public Enterprises", Report submitted to the *Ministry of France Government of Bangladesh and United Nations,* April 1986.

35. Song, Dae-lee "New Public Enterprises Policy and Efficiency Improvement", *Korean Development Institute Working Paper* No. 8811. September 1988, KDI, Seoul, South Korea.

36. Jones Leroy P, "Improving Korea's Public Enterprises Evaluation Efforts. "*Korean Development Institute, Korea,* 1985.

37. Rammurthi, Ravi "Performance Contracting System in Bangladesh "Report submitted to the *Ministry of France, Government of Bangladesh and the United Nations,* April 1986.

38. Park, Young C. "System for Evaluating the Performance of Government Invested Enterprises in the Republic of Korea", *World Bank Discussion Paper,* November 1986.

39. Jones Leroy P. "Towards a Performance Evaluation Methodology for Public Enterprises: Special Reference to Pakistan", Paper presented at the *International Symposium on Economic Performance of Public Enterprises,* Islamabad, Pakistan, 1981.

40. Mehdi, Istaqbal, "Setting Targets for Improving Cost Efficiencies In Public Enterprises", Paper presented at a *Seminar on 'Elimination of Waste through Cost Effective Management* for public enterprises in developing countries', Karachi, 1-4th July, 1985.

41. Shaikh, Hafeez, "Performance Evaluation of Public Enterprises: Lessons from the Pakistan Experience", Paper presented at the *Association of Indian Economic Studies (AIES),* New Orleans, December 1986.

42. Sankar, T. L., Mishra, R. K., Nandagopal, R, "MOU's for the State Level Public Enterprises in India", *Economic and Political Weekly,* August 31st, 1991.

43. Vernon, Raymond "Linking Managers with Ministries: Dilemma's of the SOE'S" *Journal of Policy Analysis and Management,* Volume 4, No. 1, 1984.

44. Mallon, Richard, D. "Performance Contracts with State Owned Public Enterprises", *Development Discussion Paper* No. 143, Harvard Institute for International Development, February 1983.

45. Beesely, M. E., Likierneas, A, Bloomfield, S. " Commentaries on State Enterprise Control Problems", Discussion Paper No. 302, *Economic Council of Canada,* Ontario.

46. Menon, Krishna, Umapathy, Srinivasa, "Control Systems for SOE'S: Conceptual Framework", Working Paper No. 5/85, *School ofManagement Working* Paper Series, Boston University.

47. Shirley, Mary M. "Contracts Between the State and It's Enterprises", The Experience of France & Senegal, *World Bank Staff Working Papers* on Managing State Owned Enterprises, No. 577, Washington, 1983.

48. Shirley, Mary, M. "Contracts Between the State and It's Enterprises", The Experience of France & Senegal, *World Bank Staff Working Papers* on Managing State Owned Enterprises, No. 577, Washington, 1983.

49. Department of Development and Support Management Services, United Nations, New York, 1995.

50. *Bureaucrats in Business,* Oxford University Press, 1995.

51. *A Handbook for Managers:* Commonwealth Secretariat, United Nations. New York, 1995.

6

Board Dynamics in Public Enterprises: Challenges Ahead

–R.. K. Mishra & B. Navin

Since the announcement of the new economic policy in July 1991, the restructuring of the institution of board of directors has held centrestage in the reform policy of the government with regard to the central public enterprises (CPEs). Earlier the Krishna Menon Committee (1959), Administrative Reforms Commission (1967), Fazal Mohammed Committee (1983), Economic Administration Commission (1983) and Arjun Sengupta Committee (1984) had advocated far fetched changes in this respect[1] The present paper makes an attempt to portray the dynamics of public enterprise boards and to study the impact of the changing policy of the government thereon.

Methodology

A questionnaire on changing role of board of directors in the context of new economic policy was circulated to 246 central public enterprises to elicit information of the different facets of the dynamics of public enterprise boards. 35 enterprises spanning various cognate groups comprising manufacturing and service units responded. The findings of the study are stated below:

Personal Profile

In the case of 21 CPEs, the CEOs were in the age group of 55-60 years. Among others, these enterprises included CMC–a Hi-Tech enterprise BDL-a vital defence enterprise, ONGC, VSNL and MTNL. 9 enterprises had their CEOs in the age group of 50-55 years. ANTRIX and HVOC had their CEOs in the age group of 45-50. The former operates in the field of space technology and the latter faces cut throat competition in the field of edible oils. ECL–a provider of educational consultancy, MFL- fertlisers and NSC– seeds had their CEOs in the age group of 40-45 years (Table 6.1).

Table 6.1 : Personal Data

Age Groups	*Number*	*Name of the Enterprises*
40-45	3	ECL, MFL, NSC
45-50	2	ANTRIX, HVOC
50-55	9	BEL, BPCL, GSYL, HLL, MECL, NHPC, SCIL, SIIL, STC
55-60	21	BCPL, BDL, CMC, CMPDL, GRSE, HAL, HFCL, HPCL, ITI, MAPL, MTNL, MDL, NALCO, NEPA, NPC, NSICL, ONGC, RCFL, TCIL, VSNL, WPLS

Source: Compiled from responses to questionnaire.

The age profile of the CEOs brings out some interesting conclusions. One, the top brass of CPEs is ageing. In contrast to present global trends of appointing CEOs in the age group of 35-45 years, the government still puts premium to the age factor in the appointment of CEOs in CPEs. Two, the relatively recent CPEs set up during the 1980s and 1990s have younger CEOs Finally, the government has started appreciating the fact that the hi-tech, knowledge based and competitive enterprises need younger CEOs.

The experience profile of CEOs as a board member reveals that 18 CEOs had 0-3 years experience as a board member (Table 6.2). An equal number of CEOs had experience ranging between 3-24 years. Coming to the CEOs' experience on the private and public sector boards, it is observed that 20 CEOs had 3 years or less experience in public sector. 15 CEOs had 3-12 years experience on public sector boards. On the other hand, 31 CEOs had 3 years or less experience in private sector. Only 4 CEOs had 3-15 years experience on the private sector boards.

Table 6.2: Experience of CEOs as a Board Member

Experience (yrs.)	*No. of CEOs in Public*	*No. of CEOs in Private*	*No. of CEOs in Total*
0-3	20	31	18
3-6	6	3	6
6-9	4	0	6
9-12	5	0	4
12-15	0	1	0
21-24	0	0	1

Source: Compiled from responses to questionnaire.

The analysis points to the fact that in the zone of 0-3 years of experience, more number of CEOs had experience on private sector boards as compared to public sector. In the higher experience zones, the CEOs had comparatively less experience of being on the private sector boards. It is clear from the above that the inbreeding of CEOs in CPEs is now recognised as a major limitation to their further growth. This is paving the way for recruitment from private sector.

The CEOs is the hub of the corporate wheel. His contribution can make or mar the performance of an enterprise. The CEOs identified their contribution under some common focus areas such as targeting performance, R & D, ethics, JVs, export policies, restructuring HRD, Business strategy budget estimates, draft MOU, industrial relations, productivity, rationalisation of labour, leadership, work ethics, indigenisation, export development, diversification, SWOT, customer focus, radical changes, turnover, fabrication, physical and financial performance, greater freedom for board, induction of non-government officials, revival package, removal of bottlenecks in capacity utilisation, strategic decision-making. Table 6.3 shows that the contribution was more prominent in operational and routine areas. The CEOs could not pride themselves in areas such as corporate culture building, creation of a new regime of values and ethics and transforming public enterprises into self sustained organisations. 9 out of 35 enterprises (26 percent) viz, ANTRIX, BCPL, BDL, MFL, HPCL, HVOC, MAPL and NSICL and WPCS chose not to respond as to what was the most valuable contribution made by the CEOs during their tenure.

Table 6.3: Contribution as Board Member

Name of the Enterprise	*Most Important Contribution as Board Member*
1	*2*
1. ANTRIX	No Response
2. BCPL	No Response
3. BDL	No Response
4. BEL	Targeting performance; R&D; ethics; JVs; export policy
5. BPCL	Restructuring
6. CMC	Restructuring; business strategy; HRD
7. CMPDL	GIS; conputerisation of geological modeling; HRD
8. ECL	Budget estimates; draft MOU
9. GRSE	Industrial relations; provudicity; rationalisation of labour
10. GSYL	Leadership; work ethics; nation building
11. HAL	Indigenisation; diversification; export development
12. HFCL	No Response
13. HLL	Diversification; industrial relations; overall performance
14. HPCL	No Response
15. HVOC	No Response
16. ITI	Trunover, sorted pending issues with DOT
17. MAPL	No Response
18. MECL	Radical changes; open mgt. & commitment; customer focusj computerisation
19. MTNL	SWOT of MTNL;Mission 2000, $ 418 million GDR issue
20. MDL	Fabrication; inastllation of 11 well head platforms-ONGC-Neelam Project
21. MFL	No Response
22. NALCO	Physical & financial performance
23. NEPA	Product diversification; skilful fund mgt.; turn around of the sick unit
24. NHPC	Greater freedom for teh Board, induction of non-govt. officials; greater delegation of power with increased responsibility & accountability
25. NPC	Removal of bottlenecks in capacity utilisation; effecting organisational changes
26. NSC	Diversification; production of high vale crops
27. NSICL	No Response

1	2
28. ONGC	Policy changes; development of new sources of energy like CBM and gas hydrate
29. RCFL	Performance improvement & introducing discipline
30. SCIL	Consolidation of efforts to maintain profitability
31. SIIL	Felicitating decision-making process at Board level; total participatory process; agenda in advance
32. STC	Responsible for the turn around of Projects and Equipments Corporation of India Ltd.
33. TCIL	Formation of revival package for the sick unit TCIL; induction of JV
34. VSNL	Overall mgt. and strategic direction of VSNL
35. WPCS	No Response

Source: Compiled from responses to questionnaire.

Board Composition and Board Meetings

That the government lacked the understanding of the role that boards could play in public enterprises is seen from the fact that 14 enterprises (40 per cent of the sample enterprises) had vacancies on their boards to the tune of more than 50 percent. Table 6.4 shows that 17 enterprises (about 49 percent) had vacancies in the zone of 20-50 percent.

Table 6.4 : Vacancy Position in the Board

% Vacancy	*No. of Enterprises*	*Name of the Enterprise*
0-25	4	BDL (20), BEL (0), CMC (0), SCIL (14)
20-50	17	CMPDL (47), ECIL (42), GRJE (27), HAL (33), HFCL (33), ITI (27), MDL (33), MFL (35), NALCO (42), NHPC (33), NPCL (36), NSC (31), SIIL (25), NPC (36), STC (43), WPCS (25)
Above 50	14	ANTRIX (38), BCPL (50), HLL (50), HPCL (58), IOC (67), MAPL (50), MECL (58), MTNL (58), NEPA (58), RIPL (50), ONGC (52), TCIL (65), VSNL (58)

Source: Compiled from responses to questionnaire.

Table 6.5:Composition Internal Vs. Government Nominees

Composition (% of the present size of the Board)	*No. of Enterprises (% of Total)*
	Internal Members
0-50%	24(68%)
>50	11(32%)
	Government Nominees
0-50%	25 (71.1)
>50	10(29%)

Source: Compiled from responses to questionnaire.

Table 6.5 shows that 10 enterprises (29 percent) had government nominees exceeding 50 per cent of the board strength whereas 25 enterprises (71 percent) had government nominees turning out to be 50 percent or less. 34 enterprises (97 percent) were not in favour of increasing the presence of government nominees. Against the optimal number of 12 members suggested for effective corporate governance, the average size over the 6 year period turned out to be 7 in the case of enterprises under the study with the average composition as given in Table 6.6 below:

Table 6.6 : Average Composition

Average Composition of Board	*Number of Members*
Internal	3
Workers' Representatives	0
Government Nominees	3
Nominees from FIs	1
Ex-Officio Members	0
External Professionals	0
Others	0

Source: Compiled from responses to questionnaire.

As per the Articles of Association of the responding boards they should hold atleast once in three months a board meeting. The new land marks suggested by the various committees referred to earlier indicate once a month meeting as an ideal frequency. The analysis of the frequency of board meetings of the enterprises under study shows that board meetings averaged to 7 per year.

The indifference towards recognition of the boards as an instrumentality of corporate governance was displayed not only by the government but also by the corporate management at the enterprise level. This is evidenced from Table 6.7 which shows the availability of agenda for board meeting to the members of public enterprise boards. 4 enterprises (11 percent) sent the agenda papers less than a week before the board meeting whereas 21 enterprises (60 percent) sent the agenda papers just a week before. 24 CEOs (about 69 percent) felt that board members gave constructive suggestions and 11 CEOs (31 percent) indicated that it was only sometimes that the board members made value addition. In 13 (37 percent) cases, the member of the boards were not consulted on the preparation of the agenda for the board meeting. In an equal number of cases they were only casually consulted in the formulation of agenda and in 9 cases (26 percent) they were not at all consulted. On an average the government boards discussed 2:3 routine items to new items and 3:4 policy to operational issues.

Table 6.7 : Availability of Agenda for Board Meeting

No. of days in Advance	*No. of Enterprises in Percentage*
Less than 7	14
7	63
10	1
15	22

Source: Compiled from responses to questionnaire.

Corporate Governance

The governing boards are the most important link in the chain as their proactiveness is an important element to stir other elements. These boards have to a clear vision about their role, the role of the government nominees, appointment of subject committees for their improved functioning and evaluation of the contribution of the CEO and other board members. Table 6.8 shows the role of governing boards in the responding public enterprises. The HVOC equated the objectives mentioned in their Memorandum of Association and Articles of Association with the role it's board plays. ANTRIX and SCIL were not forthcoming on this issue. NSC had carved out a role on practical and operational aspects for its board. MDL confined the role of the board to setting up targets of production, its review and assessment of capacity utilisation.

Table 6.8 : Role of Board of Directors

Name of the Enterprise	*Role of the BoDs (Formal & Informal)*
1	*2*
1. ANTRIX	—
2. BCPL	Overall policy guidelines: to help the company to prepare long range plans, appointment of key managers.
3. BDL	Board will have to be cohesive and play a progressive role in shaping the destiny of the company.
4. BEL	Setting corporate machine, objectics, goals, reviewing the performance, framing corporate policies and conducting SWOT analysis.
5. BPCL	Setting the companies strategic aim, providing leadership, supervising management of the business, reporting to sharholders on Board's/stewardship.
6. CMC	Guidelines of DPE should only be guidelines and not rules. Board should have powers to look into salary prequisites, profitability, etc.
7. CMPDL	Advising and guiding the Board, cautioning the board about pitfalls.
8. ECL	To provide directions for growth of the company and monitor progress in constructive manner.
9. GRSE	Board must be the supreme policy making body to manage the company in the best interest of the enterprise. Government should not try to do backseat driving through nominated directors.

1	*2*
10. GSYL	Chairman should take the decision with informal/formal advice from the Board.
11. HAL	Policy formulation and updating review, monitor implementation of plans, ensure compliance of laws, guide in technology updation, give fillip to R&D effort, monitor progress of new projects/diversification programmes.
12. HFCL	Give their view points and benefit of their experience in taking major policy decision.
13. HLL	BoD should be able to give professional guidance to the corporate body.
14. HPCL	Directors should meet in Board meetings to approve various growth oriented agenda with pragmatic views in regard to size, nature and tough external competition.
15. HVOC	As under MoA and AoA.
16. ITI	Formulation of policy guidelines, superintendence, formation of JVCs, foreign collaboration.
17. MAPL	To manage business of the company by exercising all such powers within the framework of the Companies Act.
18. MECL	To guide the company towards gorwth in today's competitive market, lay down policies and monitor its implementation.
19. MTNL	BoD should give a feedback on the performance of the company based on the knoweldge and interaction with the members of the public.
20. MDL	role of the Board should be confined to setting up targets of production in terms of quantity and value; review of actual production vis-a-vis targets; assessment of under utilisation of capacity by determining attainable production vis-a-vis firm orders/projected demand; prescription of standards of equipment utilisation, broad targets of inventory levels.
21. MFL	Board should monitor executive management; should present a balanced and understandable assessment of company's position; should estabish an audit committee;, should devote time and effort to attend meetings.

1	*2*
22. NALCO	To set goals, to set overall policies, to decide strategies for future.
23. NEPA	To guide senior level management on policy matters; interact with ministries in government and other agencies to further development of the organisation. General image building for the company in different flora.
24. NHPC	Board should guide the organisation in the short and long term plans. Extend advice and assistance in technical, financial, administrative and organisational matters to ensure best performance. Board should be a vocal mouth piece to project corporation's achievements and aspirations and protect the same from adverse actions and reactions from various quarters.
25. NPC	BoD should be mainly concerned with formulation of policy and to review the performance of the on-going projects, performance of the operating stations and exercise the powers which are vested in the BoD with regard to sanctions and approvals.
26. NSC	More concentration on practical perational aspects. Free and frank brain storming discussions. Each and ever director should be heard.
27. NSICL	Board should be available to visualise the future scenario and direct accordingly the future activities. Monitor aspiration of the service user, general economy and employees to give proper policy direction. Adopt techniques of successful managerial practices of private sector boards.
28. ONGC	Develop a long lasting vision of the company. Provide strategic direction, promote business and ensure long-term growth, and value in large investment decisions, encourage creativity, technology up-gradation and value based business.
29. RCFL	BoD is the pivotal authority created by the company. Role is mainly in laying down policies and ensure strategic and long-term plans are carried out. Role is insignificant in the field of development and creation of core competence.
30. SCIL	No response.

1	*2*
31. SIIL	Assist company through their inputs in strategic planning, provide support in controlling external environment. Provide guidance and bridge in the knowledge gap in areas like technical/marketing. Finance/ HR/Operations.
32. STC	Formulation of corporate plan/policies/strategies. Fixation of targets and laying down of control/monitoring mechanism.
33. TCIL	to evolve strategic plan, its implementation monitoring.
34. VSNL	A combination of formal and informal roles is desirable. The board members may if need be have to formal advance discussions to arrive at formal decisions.
35. WPCS	The directors in the respective professional field apart from dwelling on board proceedings shall also share the responsibility to develop strategies and plan for business development and to be proactive in resolving key issues in the implemenation process. This interaction shall be through a sub-committee which shall function under the CMD and report to the Board from time to time.

Source: Compiled from responses to questionnaire.

That the governing boards had less than an adequate idea of corporate governance is seen from the fact that 14 enterprises (40 percent) did not appoint sub-committees. The various models suggested on the formation of sub-committees provide a space for the inclusion of non-board members. They do not insist on every committee being headed by the CEOs. In the case of the central enterprises the members of the committees in most cases are the CEOs, directors from various functional areas, representatives of government and thin representation of management experts. In 21 out of 35 enterprises (60 percent), the committees focused on R & D, projects, share issue and transfer, delegation of power, financial restructuring and pay revision. These committees once on an average met once a month.

Managerial Succession Planning

In 77 per cent cases (27 out of 35 enterprises), there was awareness about managerial succession planning whereas in the remaining cases no succession planning existed. The succession planning process is said to be based on the merit experience and competency for vacancies arising out of either retirement, growth, new business etc. It is planning atleast 6 months in advance in most of the cases and in some case even 2 years in advance. Successors at each level are identified and transferred at the appropriate time. In some cases succession takes place by induction or appointing as an understudy to the serving officer. For board level appointments, Public Enterprise Selection Board (PESB) plays a major role. Even in the case of second level officers, PESB is involved in appointments. Though the responding public enterprises in general claimed to have a managerial succession planning, the annual surveys on the working of public enterprises published by the department of public enterprise for the various years reveal that atleast 25 per cent of the CEO positions remain vacant at any point of time

PESB being the body for finalising the board level appointments is required to ensure that CPEs do not remain topless. In 15 out of 25 (43 per cent cases) CPEs, the respondents feel that PESB has significantly contributed towards the succession planning whereas 9 out of 35 (26 per cent) feel its contribution is moderate. Only one enterprise feels that its contribution has been great. 21 out of 35 CPEs (60 per cent) feel that PESB requires restructuring. The rest 14 feel that it is not required. 13 out of 35 enterprises (37 per cent) feel that the composition of second level committee is moderately balanced. 3 out of 35 enterprises (8 per cent) feel it is least balanced. 23 enterprises (71 per cent) feel that there is a need to bring about a change in the role of PESB. The same number of enterprises think that PESB should be made an autonomous body and given full powers (Table 6.9). This shows that CPEs prefer PESB to continue but in a restructured way. This is reinforced by the finding that 27 enterprises (77 per cent) are against boards for electing their own chiefs themselves. The general view about the board level appointments is that the CEO with his experience of the unit should have a say in the selection of the board members as well as the CEO. PESB should not depend on the administrative Ministry to initiate the selection process. PESB selections should be final. The clearance from the Cabinet Committee on Appointments should not take more than a month.

Table 6.9 : PESB Performance

PESB Performance	*Restructuring*	*Balance of Composition of PESB's Second Level Selection Committee*	*PESB Role*	*PESB Autonomy*
Significant (43%)	Yes (60%)	Significant (54%) 19 / 25	Change (29%)	Pro (68%)
Excellent (30%)	No (40%)	Moderate (37%) 13 / 35	No change (71%)	Anti (32%)
Moderate (26%)	—	Least (8%) 3 / 35	—	—
No Response (28%)	—	—	—	—

Source: Compiled from responses to questionnaire.

Conclusion

The new economic policy mentions reform in the institution of board of directors in CPEs as one of the main planks of public enterprise restructuring. The institution of board of directors determines the destiny of an enterprise[2]. The research on board of directors of 35 CPEs reveals several facets of their malfunctioning. The Boards are not only ageing but also suffer from heavy inbreeding. This ill-equips CPEs to face domestic and global competition. The analysis of the frequency of board meeting of the enterprises under study shows that board meetings averaged to 7 per year. 60 percent of the board level positions remained vacant. The boards suffer from excessive presence of government officials and the other nominated members. In 29 per cent cases, the government nominees exceeded more than 50 per cent of board strength. Their domination was so intense that 97 per cent of the sample enterprises turned down the idea of increasing their strength on public enterprise boards. In 77 per cent cases the agenda for board meeting was provided within 7 days of the date of the board meeting. 40 per cent of the sample enterprises did not set up board committees. 23 per cent of the CPEs did not have a managerial succession planning system and 60 per cent of the respondents were for restructuring the role of the PESB. 37 per cent of the CPEs felt that the balance of composition of PESB's second level selection committee was moderate. 68 per cent felt that PESB should be provided greater autonomy. The corporate governance function was in low key. The CEOs lacked a clear vision. 9 sample enterprises were not able to state the single most important contribution of their CEOs. To sum up there is an urgent need to revamp the boards of CPEs to make them business like, organic, competitive and future driven.

Abbreviations

1. ANTRIX	Antrix Corporation Ltd.
2. BCPL	Bengal Chemicals & Pharmaceuticals Ltd.
3. BDL	Bharat Dynamics Ltd.
4. BEL	Bharat Electronics Ltd.
5. BPCL	Bharat Petroleum Corporation Ltd.
6. CMC	Computer Maintenance Corporation Ltd.
7. CMPDL	Central Mine Planning & Design Institute Ltd.
8. ECL	Educational Consultants India Ltd.
9. GRSE	Garden Reach Shipbuilders and Engineers Ltd.
10. GSYL	Goa Ship Yard Ltd.
11. HAL	Hindustan Aeronautics Ltd.
12. HFCL	Hindustan Fertilizer Corporation Ltd.
13. HLL	Hindustan Latex Ltd.
14. HPCL	Hindustan Paper Corporation Ltd.
15. HVOC	Hindustan Vegetable Oils Corporation Ltd.
16. ITI	Indian Telephone Industry
17. MAPL	Maharashtra Antibiotics and Pharamaceuticals Ltd.
18. MECL	Mineral Exploration Corporation Ltd.
19. MTNL	Mahanagar Telephone Nigan Ltd.
20. MDL	Mazagaon Dock Ltd.
21. MFL	Madras Fertilizers Ltd.
22. NALCO	National AluminiumCompany Ltd.
23. NEPA	
24. NHPC	National Hydroelectric Power Corporation Ltd.
25. NPC	Nuclear Power Corporation Ltd.
26. NSC	National Seeds Corporation Ltd.
27. NSICL	National Small Industries Corporation Ltd.
28. ONGC	Oil and Natural Gas Corporation Ltd.
29. RCFL	Rashtriya Chemicals & Fertilisers Ltd.
30. SCIL	Shipping Corporation of India Ltd.
31. SIIL	Sponge Iron India Ltd.
32. STC	State Trading Corporation of India Ltd.
33. TCIL	Tyre Corporation of India Ltd.
34. VSNL	Videsh Sanchar Nigam Ltd.
35. WPCS	Water & Power Consultancy Services (I) Ltd.

References

1. R.K. Mishra, "*India: Country Study*", in John Corkery, Colm O Nullian and Roger Wettenhall (ed), 'Public Enterprise Boards: What They Are and What They Do', International Association of Schools and Institutes of Administrations, 1994, Brussels, pp. 55-78.
2. R.K. Mishra "Public Enterprise Policy in India", Kaliedo Scope, Standing Conference on Public Enterprises, Aug-Sept. 1999, New Delhi, p. 11.

7

Competitiveness of Public Sector in India

— *R.K.Mishra*

India is in throes of a rapid economic transition. The past record of the country can only be of marginal support to help it write new economic equation, entitling it to march to a new millenium and realise the visualisation that its founding fathers had stated in the Directive Principles of the Indian Constitution. The country has to prepare itself for the fundamental economic transformation not only to join the group of economies leading the world, but also to develop a new self-adjusting framework providing continuous opportunity to its economy for organic growth. Competitiveness, is the litmus test in the present era of globalisation and internationalisation. All sectors of any economy have to qualify in this test. Public sector in India, cannot be an exception to this.

The purpose of this paper is to discuss the significance of competitiveness in public sector to the Indian economy; its present orientation with regard to competitiveness; status of its competitiveness and measures to make it internationally competitive. Public sector is an amorphous term. It includes in its scope, Government departments, departmental enterprises and autonomous public enterprises. The present paper, takes into consideration only the last category of public sector.

Further, public enterprises in India include both the Central public enterprises (CPEs) and the State level enterprises (SLPEs). According to some studies, even the enterprises owned and managed by the local bodies are included within the ambit of public enterprises. For the purpose of the present paper, we have mostly dealt with the CPEs. However, reference has been made to the SLPEs wherever necessary. Public enterprise is a vast economic aggregate. We have therefore referred to sectoral or individual cases to drive home our point.

Why Competitiveness?

Competitiveness is a basic element of the new economic paradigm endorsed by market economy framework and global institutions. Competitiveness optimises allocative efficiency and provides sinews for self-sustained growth. Competitiveness is taken to mean a higher growth in turnover and market share, value-addition, technology adoption on the one hand and relative efficiency on the cost and price fronts on the other.

Public enterprises in India, employ an investment of Rs. 5,00,000 crore composed of Rs. 2,00,000 crore in the CPEs, Rs. 2,00,000 crore in the SLPEs and Rs. 1,00,000 crore in the departmental and local level public enterprises. They contribute to about 45% of the capital formation. There are 243 CPEs, 1100 SLPEs and about 100 departmental and local level enterprises. Much of the technological transformation that has taken place in the country has come through these enterprises. The wide and diversified range of goods manufactured and services provided by these enterprises include, bakery products, coal, steel, transport and power, automobiles, heavy electrical equipment, life and general insurance, banking, educational consultancy and trading. There is hardly any major sector of economic activity where public sector is not present. It is therefore necessary that public enterprise in India acquire competitive orientation to put the country on a new trajectory. Unless this happens, we cannot join the club of countries achieving self propelled growth.

India being a mixed economy, the inputs provided by public sector are used as raw materials or intermediate goods by the private sector. The public-private sector mix is undergoing a change in the favour of the latter, implying thereby the fundamental necessity of the public sector to remain competitive. The globalisation and internationalisation, strongly call for the need of India's public sector to inculcate competitiveness for two reasons: (1) Indian businesses cannot internationalise their operations as long as they do not possess the required competitive advantage and (2) the inputs provided by the Indian businesses should not make the exports/production in the home country disadvantageous.

Public enterprises in India have grown in a protectionist framework. They very cleverly devised creative financial strategies and technical efficiency parameters to ensure their survival. They justified their continuation in the name of import substitution. The concepts such as economic resource protection (ERP) and domestic resource saving (DRS) were used to support their operations. This could not stand valid for long as these could not substitute the price competitiveness. With the opening up of the economy, now they face an increased threat from the private sector and global economic forces. These enterprises have to devise perforce a new analytical framework to evaluate the effectiveness of their operations. Unless they opt for such a change their existence is wide exposed to the competitive forces. Their failure is likely to upset the national apple-carte resulting in a setback to dominant aggregates such as employment, demand, savings, exports, current account deficit and fiscal deficit to mention a few.

Competitive Orientation and Status

This section deals with the extent of present orientation of public enterprises towards competitiveness taking into account parameters such as accounting and financial practices, operations management, labour, cost and research & development. As attempt is made to understand whether public enterprises have domestic or global market orientation. This is supplemented by a study of factors responsible for such orientation.

The accounting and financial practices adhered to by these enterprises are by and large based on the framework developed by nodal institutions such as the Institute of Chartered Accountants of India, Institute of Cost and Works Accountants of India, Institute of

Chartered Secretaries, Ministry of Finance, Reserve Bank of India, Securities and Exchange Board of India etc. The content of accounting and financial policies is largely influenced by some legislations such as the Indian Companies Act, Banking Companies and Regulations Act and the Enabling Acts under which the statutory corporations were set up. The Department of Public Enterprise, had set up a group on accounting practices on public enterprises in early 1990s. The group endorsed the accounting concepts and conventions adopted by the Institute of Chartered Accountants of India. Of the innumerable generally agreed accounting principles, adopted by the International Accounting Standards Board, only a few have been adopted by the Institute of Chartered Accountants of India. This has acted as a barrier for getting listed on the International bourses such as the New York Stock Exchange (NYSE) or the Luxembourg Stock Exchange or the City. A company is required to disclose information on 84 parameters in the case of the NYSE as compared to about 15 in the case of the Bombay Stock Exchange. The weekly balance sheets and profit and loss statements have to be provided in the case of the NYSE. Most of the American companies place their financial statements on the Internet. During 1996-97, 76 CPEs did not either publish their accounts in time or repeated the previous financial year's balances for inclusion in the Public Enterprise Survey brought out by the Department of Public Enterprise. In the case of some SLPEs, wide discrepancies are found between the figures reported for an accounting period and the text connected to the financial statements. In the case of some SLPEs, though the accounts were duly certified by the Internal Auditor, Commercial Auditor, Statutory Auditor and the Comptroller & Auditor General of India, the two sides of the Balance Sheet did not match when figures were computerised. Some CPEs follow inconsistent accounting policies. They twist the policies to present an exaggeratedly sound financial picture. The Oill and Natural Gas Commission Ltd., and the IPCL, and several other enterprises have been held accountable for this lapse. Most of the enterprises do not revalue their assets and provide for contingent liabilities. They resort to unfair practices of exaggerating turnover and profits.

In the case of SLPEs, the accounts are not prepared and finalised in time. They have been found to remain in arrears for a period of 1-17 years. The internal audit virtually does not exist. In a study commissioned by the Power Finance Corporation at the behest of the World Bank, it was revealed that the internal audit departments in the State Electricity Boards are either non-existent or dormant. They are staffed by unqualified and untrained personnel[1].

The cost norms have not been developed by many CPEs. Similarly, the cost audit is not effective. The variance analysis is not carried out periodically and there is an indifference towards analysing the causes of variance and initiating remedial action to rectify such causes. The materials cost and the associated wastages are found high. The energy costs exceed optimum levels. For instance, as against 7%-8% of energy costs, in the private sector, the CPEs have recorded energy costs of about 12%. The energy audit in the case of Mishra Dhatu Nigam Ltd. revealed three time more the consumption of energy than warranted. Excessive stocks of stores and spares are maintained to prevent standstill. The labour costs are abnormally high in the range of 12%-15% on an average. High profit earning enterprises are associated with low labour costs, howering around 5% and less of the turnover. Though the global insurance and banking industry incur less than three percent as wage and salary costs, the Indian insurance and banking industry incur a high level of wage and service cost of about 15%. There is a universal trend to adopt full cost pricing. The new technique such as incremental costing, activity based costing and strategic costing have still to find a wider acceptance. The costing decisions sometime overlook even the fundamental concept of contribution. If these were to be applied in time, a large chunk of enterprises would have made sound costing decisions and ensured the continuation of a large gamut of such activities which had a positive contribution over a period of time.

Instances are galore where unhealthy financial practices are followed. There have been instances of using discretion to the ultimate disadvantage of the enterprise. To circumvent the payment of dividend and to show a high earnings per share (EPS), funds were shown by an enterprise as advance made towards equity. The Debt-Equity ratios increased the financial risk so much so that some public enterprises lost all their gross margin to meet the interest charge and thereby turn into the red. As opposed to this, in some cases excessive equity was provided leaving the enterprise unable to make the balancing act to approach the capital market on account of abnormally high proportions of debt. The National Aluminium Company Limited is attempting an exercise for the reversal of such a pattern. The Steel Authority of India Limited (SAIL) has been engaged in such exercise for quite some time. In fact, the concept of one time debt-equity ratio stands discredited now and enterprises go on changing this in search of the optimum. Though some of the CPEs are corporate majors, they have not been listed on the Indian bourses to encourage trading in the shares of disinvested enterprises. The Government of India and the Securities & Exchange Board of India (SEBI) required them to get listed. However, many such enterprises pleaded their inability to comply with the exhaustive listing norms. SEBI responded quite well to their requests and relaxed the conditions by prescribing the requirement of filling up a brief listing document. About 20 enterprises only have taken advantage of such relaxation. That the cost of capital and the associated financial risks have not received due attention, is amply evident from the fact that the Economic Value Added (EVA) has been negative or very paltry in these enterprises.

Public enterprises suffer from rampant over-manning. The total deposits of the commercial banking system in India is about Rs. 9,00,00 crore. This sector employs about three lakh personnel. The Bank of Belgium, headquartered at Brussels, manages a deposit of 10,00,000 crore with about 10,000 personnel. The quantity of steel produced by SAIL by 3 lakh employees, is produced by similar organisations globally be about 30,000 employees. The Indian enterprises in general have been found lower in the realm of Human Resource Development (HRD) on vocational training, skilled labour, productivity linked wages, worker motivation, labour flexibility, managerial initiative and management education. This holds true even with public enterprises. It has been found that in the case of lower levels of management, no worthwhile plans are formulated especially at the shop floor level and supervisory levels to train them. Even executives at the junior, middle and senior levels are not sent for training to the best enterprises in their respective fields. Very little time is spent on training top management and the money spent on training is not treated as worthwhile investment. Bharat Heavy Electricals Limited (BHEL) example of accounting of human resources needs to be emulated by the rest. The labour flexibility has not made inroads mainly because of indifference to multi-skilling and appropriate HRD administration. Flexi-timings have not been introduced. Managerial empowerment has not received much attention. For instance, even in the case of corporate planning and the MOU, the bottom up or top down approaches have not received the due attention. The public sector wage committees including the Mohan Committee and the Ranganath Mishra Committee paid scant regard to productivity linked wages. In Japan, USA and several other countries, basic wages is a very small component of the overall wage structure. The performance linked wages are a crucial component of the total wages. The application of this system in the case of the Jaipur Metals & Electricals Ltd. — A Government of Rajasthan Cooperative Enterprise, transformed it from a sick to a financially healthy enterprise.

The absence of hire and fire has also led to low productivity. Article 12 of the Indian Constitution, deprives a public enterprise to benefit from this system. The new development such as issuance of stock options or performance based rewards and promotions, barring a few enterprises are yet to be introduced. Management education is considered a good investment proposal by reputed corporates. In Japan, the chief executive has to spend one-third of his total time in management education and development. Though there are about sixty in-house training institutions in the case of CPEs, their functioning does not qualify for much appreciation. Some of them are extinct and non-operational. The huge enterprises like BHEL, SAIL, Coal companies etc., could have collaborated with management institutions to launch suitable educational; programmes. Recently, the Indian Bankers Association, is collaborating with the India Gandhi National Open University, to launch a three-year post experience programme in banking for its fellow members.

Operations management provides a great leeway for developing competitiveness. First comes the question of technique. Instead of production by shifts public enterprises could plan their production through group technology and continuous production schemes. They may even like to outsource some of their operations or go in for global location of their production facility. The National Mineral Development Corporation (NMDC) is planning to buy mines in Zimbabwe. The designing and engineering aspects pull down public enterprises in terms of excellence and call for good deal of learning. The vendor selection, vendor development and supplier relationship are the parameters on which public enterprises are competitively very low. The importance of supply chain management is yet to be realised. The operatonalisation of this concept can help public enterprises in both the project implementation stage and when the project is on stream. The maintenance is another neglected aspect. The public sector jute mills in Tripura have to wait for months to get stores and spares air-lifted from Calcutta for maintenance. The poor maintenance of aircrafts by the Indian Airlines and Air India cutting into effective operationalisation of flight schedules is a well-known fact.

Pubic enterprises are found to be abysmally low on marketing. The growth of turnover is static. Normally their capital employed to turnover ratio is 1:1 as against 1:3 in the case of the private sector enterprises and 5:1 recorded globally. Their market shares are stagnant. Though 20% of the foreign trade (exports) is through the public enterprises, most of it relates to the canalised items. The exports are of residual nature which deprives these enterprises to have a flavour of the developments in the international markets. The international comparison of customer orientation of enterprises in India shows that we are the among the lowest, in product quality, product design, on time delivery, after sales service and managing distribution. The Central and the State level public enterprises conform to these findings. Recently the Steel Authority of India

Ltd. was charged with producing inferior quality steel. Several exporters have complained in the past about defective designs of the products of BHEL. A number of public enterprises have been held responsible for non delivery of goods in time. The poor after sales service was responsible for the steep fall in the sales of consumer electronics and refrigerators produced by Electronics Corporation of India Ltd. and Hyderabad Allwyn Ltd. respectively. The poor customer orientation of the public sector banks is reflected in the increasing volumes of business of the private sector banks. The selling & distribution concepts adopted are not suited for market penetration and maximisation of revenues.

Research & Development acts both as an engine of growth and stability. In any analysis of R&D efforts, the focus should be on developing the risk taking capacity on account of strategic changes in the market or the enterprise plans to deliberately influence the market. The analysis of the R &D scenario in public enterprises, points out that the R&D expenditure has shrunk over the years from 3% of their aggregate turnover to about 1.5% whereas it has been noted that during the nineties R&D spending has increased in private sector. There is a marked shift in the public sector spending in R&D from basic research to applied research. The case of the Indian Drugs and Pharmaceuticals Ltd. could be cited to show as to how over a period of time the company resigned its supremacy to the private sector companies by ignoring to develop patents and concentrate only on the distribution of bulk drugs.

Framework for Competitiveness

The orientation of public enterprises towards competitiveness and its status makes it evident that bold initiatives are required to be taken to permeate the competitiveness in its fullest measure. The measures to be taken could be classified as strategic, interface and internal measures.

Strategic Measures

Sankar and Mishra (1989 & 1990), in their initial[2] and modified[3] matrix suggested the reorganisation of public sector businesses along core and non-core activities. They advocated that enterprises successful in financial terms and operating in competitive markets could be privatised, whereas enterprises unsuccessful in financial terms and markets could be privatised, whereas enterprises unsuccessful in financial terms and operating in competitive markets could be wound up. Enterprises falling in other categories need to be restructured. The Rangarajan Committee[4] suggested departure from the concept of 100 percent ownership to zero percent to debureaucratise and degovernmentalise pubic enterprises. It suggested 26% share holdings for the State to ensure limited control over spatial resolutions brought in general body meeting of the enterprises and 51% to have effective control. It suggested 100% for full ownership. The scheme has to be operationalised giving due weightage to importance of the various public enterprises at the present juncture. The reduction of the Government's share holdings to 49% would free public enterprises from the control of 'saptarishi' and 'trishul'. However, the parliamentarians in India would do well to practice the right of self denial in tabling questions. The role of the Clerk in the U.K. parliamentary system, who is the counterpart of the Speaker in the Indian Parliament, is worth citing as he exercises a micropcopic scrutiny in permitting the questions to be asked on the floor of the House. The U.K. has also abolished the Select Committee on the Nationalized Industries. Is not the time ripe that the Indian Parliament abolishes the Committee on Public Undertakings?

To implement the recommendations of the Rangarajan Committee on disinvestment, the Disinvestment Commission was setup in 1996. The Commission has examined the question of competitiveness in public sector. Among other things, it has recommended improved systems of corporate governance and case by case modalities for disnvestments. The implementation of the recommendations of the Commission would have certainly improved their performance. The records of those CPEs having gone to market shows that they had the general tendency to out perform BSE-index. However, the indifference to the full-fledged implementation of the recommendations of the Commission coupled with the Government's decision of disinvestment by the public sector financial institutions has depressed their share values and their prices are not moving in tandem with the BSE-index[8].

The question of reorganisation of public sector businesses calls for a study of further division of activity of each enterprise into core and non-core, amalgamations and mergers of public enterprises, partnerships-alliances-linkages with national and international firms creating a pool of common facilities for research, manpower selection and recruitment, sharing of costs and distribution facilities. The size of an enterprise is emerging as a dominant factor[5]. The recent move to set up Petro-Net is an excellent attempt to synergise the activities of the public sector petroleum industry and help the private sector firms in this arena. The recent moves to promote cross-holdings in the equities of the various public sector oil firms is being seen as an effective step to link the upstream and downstream businesses in the public sector oil industry. This is expected to benefit the Indian consumer and provide an alternative to many foreign countries to invite Indian expertise to collaborate with their indigenous industry. The Government of Mauritius is considering to invite Indian oil majors to collaborate in preference to some well established global giants. The partnerships, alliances and linkages are expected to lift the competitiveness of the Indian Industry to the global standards. HMT Ltd. could transform its businesses by such linkages via the joint venture route. This would pave the way not only for the equity or consultancy support, but also prepare the ground for uninterrupted flow of technology and access to international markets. In the case of BHEL and BHEL type firms or SAIL, such linkages with Seimens, Inland LTV and Us Steel are likely to bring about a fundamental change in the technology governing their businesses and consequentially their customer orientation and bottom line.

The conversion of departmental enterprise and public corporations into companies would be a much sought after reform. This would put public enterprises on par with the private sector enterprises and ensure a level playing field and a healthy competition between the two. The conversion of the Indian Airlines, Air India, Industrial Development Bank of India, Industrial Finance

Corporation Bank of India and Oil and Natural Gas Commission are some cases in point. The recent price-war between the Mahanagar Telephone Nigam Ltd. and the Videsh Sanchar Nigam Ltd. on providing Internet facility supports our contention.

Policy Changes

The Government policy shapes the contours of the success of a firm. Both the Central and State Governments in India have been excessively obsessed with factors constituting the term 'public' than creating a climate favourable for discharging the 'enterprise obligations'. The "Trishul" , "Saptarishi" , guidelines issued , existing provisions of pubic accountability and Article 12 of the Indian Constitution, seriously impair not only the policy autonomy but also the functional autonomy of these enterprises. These enterprises have to take the Government's permission to import technology, establish foreign collaborations, access India and international capital markets, determine the prices of their goods and services, recruitment and fixation of pay. They cannot even change their articles and Memorandum of Association. The appointment of the Chief Executive and the composition of the Board of Directors and all nominations on such boards are done by the Government. In sum, these are not board-led undertakings. This undermines their competitiveness a great deal vis-a-vis the private sector enterprises in India and the global giants abroad. Recently the Government of India's initiative of identifying some enterprises as Navartnas and many more enterprises as Miniratnas has been a good departure form the earlier practice. The boards of the Navaratnas have been reconstituted. The first evidence of the functioning of the reconstituted boards reveals an initiation of the shift from procedures to results. However, even in the case of the reconstituted boards, there is a great scope for an enhanced and positive contribution from the Government Directors. Many disinvested companies failed to benefit from reforms because among other things their boards were not reformed. The Memorandum of Understanding (MOU) was initiated in 1987-88 to bring about a cultural and interface change in public enterprises. The number of enterprises on MOU has shot up from a mere 4 in 1987-88 to a 110 during 1996-97[6].

The system has undergone a drastic change from its initial orientation of 'contract de negotiation' to 'siganalling' system. However, in the absence of accompanying reward and punishment features, the system has not delivered the results. There is a need to examine afresh its relevance as a tool to increase competitiveness.

The guidelines issued by the Government restrained severely the freedom of public enterprises. The N. Vittal Committee[7] suggested the deletion of 762 of the 892 guidelines issued by the Government. It recommended modification of 25 guidelines and retention of only 105 guidelines. In the present context of the marketisation, there is a need to control the performance of public enterprises by results.

The policy changes cannot be a one-time measure. They have to be continuous and long term. The government of Japan enhanced the competitiveness of their enterprises for all the times to come through a series of short, medium and long- term measures. We suggest the following matrix of measures for developing competitiveness in public enterprises:

Policy Matrix for Developing Competitiveness in Indian Public Sector Enterprises

Short Term	*Medium Term*	*Long Term*
1	*2*	*3*
	Government	
* Environment scanning: niche deetermination technology monitoring. * Develop competitive incentives and instruments to guide public enterprises to new product domains. * Cordinate activities of organisations that monitor international trade, technology and competitiveness.	* Establish MITI type agency for promoting cooperation and competition in the domestic market. * Develop market – driven policy instruments rather than regulatory control to influence industry decisions. * Update the status of Institutional environment: release bureaucratic control and facilitate/ promote innovation.	* Modernise national insfrastructure for the next century. * Develop a national industrial focus. * Rethink strategies for the organisation of labour in future * Develop new mandate for scientific institutions: emphasis on commercial spin-offs and diffusion of innovation to other sectors (e.g., space, defence, etc.)

1	2	3
* Train bureaucrats in specialised fields e.g., manufacturing and services. * Develop instruments to train labour in advanced technology.	* Enforce quality standards (e.g., ISO 14000) for all domestic industrial transactions. * Develop social and environmental priorities based on domestic needs and concerns. * Promote infastructural industries. * Emphasise development of efficient logistics.	
HRD	**Institutions**	
* Update technology and management programmes by developing courses in emerging areas. * Develop cooperation between technology and management programmes. * Update skills of trainers. * Introduce extensive use of computers in curriculum. * Adopt dynamic practices based on world class services and manufacturing paradigm. * Redesign organisational structures: integration of functions in the firm and emphasise inhouse innovation. * Become more responsive to domestic consumer's needs. * Increase R and D activity in India.	* Coordinate development of technology and practices across different industries, e.g., machine tool and textiles. * Monitor trade practices within domestic producers. * Develop sectoral data banks on performance of industries. * Develop sector-focussed programmes. * Conduct joint research with industry and assist in technology transfer. * Set up pilot projects on technology innovation in conjuction with trade associations * Design consulting and training programmes for small and medium manufactures. * Set up vehicles for dissemination of knowledge in manufacturing management e.g., reserach journals, industry workshops etc.	* Develop new products and process to strengthen existing and related industries. * Play a proactive role in designing future of international trade and liaison with similar trade associations in other countries. * Setup technological parks. * Create focussed research centres and develop horizontal linkages between such centres. * Provide services to other developing nations. * Adopt global standards in evaluating performance of teachers, students and administrators.

1	2	3
* Adopt dynamic practices based on world class services and manufacturing paradigm. * Redesign organisational structures: integration of functions in the firm and emphasise inhouse innovation. * Become more responsive to domestic consumer's needs. * Increase R and D activity in India.	**Industry** * Develop expertise in strategic management of manufacturing at firm level. * Invest in updating skills of workforce in technology and managerial effectiveness. * Develop linkage with educational and reserach institutions. * Participate in the evolution of standards at ISI. * Develop environmentally viable products	* Adopt a new strategy of continuous process. * Invest in technology. * Participate in national infrastructure. * Development. * Setup focussed commercial research centres. * Develop a strategy of joint development of technology (technology consortia).

Internal Measures

A reform of the internal mechanisms may provide a gold mine to enhance the competitiveness. The optimal performance through internal action could come through systemic changes such as commercial orientation, effective management information systems, computerisation, integration of work force with organisational mission, culture building, bench marking, adherence to environmental norms and value-addition. Among these myriad of measures, we propose to expand on bench marking and value addition.

An intensive application of bench marking could act as a powerful tool to enhance competitiveness. A dissection of the financial and physical performance along some well established industry bench marks increases our understanding of the quantitative and qualitative gaps leading to rebuilding of physical and financial structures and germination of new cultural genes. For instance, any study in bench marking would reveal that energy consumption in integrated steel plants in India is far more than the Kawasaki Steel Plant, Japan. As compared to 0.8% of the total energy consumption in integrated steel plants in Japan, the integrated steel plants consume

7.84% in steel making in India. Energy accounts for about 40% of the total cost of the a steel production in India, while it is about 28% in developed countries. While most countries abroad have implemented continuous casting long ago and now 70%-100% of their steel production is by this route, India has nearly 70% of its steel production through the ingot route.

To enhance competitiveness public enterprises have to replace their engineering mentality by substitution in its place the marketing mentality which will alter the focus from achieving the targets to continuous improvements:

Types of Company Focus

Engineering Mentality New technology/viscous circle	Marketing Mentality Customer/virtuous circle
Invest in new technology	Empower Employees
↓	↓
Higher output per worker	Listen to Customer
↓	↓
More product to sell	Continous Improvement
↓	↓
Lower prices	Profitable business

The benefits that pubic enterprises can derive through value addition need to be driven home more intensively. Firstly, each activity should be taken up only in the case it adds to the value. It has been found that in the case of some public enterprises, the wage costs per employee exceed the turnover per employee. To increase competitiveness it is further necessary to study how the gains have been allocated among the different heads. What role has been played by different heads in the absolute or relative decline of value-added over a period of time. The various studies indicate a very dismal picture of creation and appropriation of value-added in pubic enterprise.

Conclusion

The competitiveness of pubic sector would determine in great measure the competitiveness of the Indian economy in the present era of globalisation and internationalisation. There is no denying the fact that the public sector suffers from a low degree of competitive orientation. On the various parameters of competitiveness it is found to lag behind vis-a-vis the private sector in India and global giants. There is a need to initiate strategic, interface and internal reforms to make Indian public enterprises the front runners in the competitiveness race. This alone is likely to sustain the ongoing liberalisation process.

References

1. R.K. Mishra, "Internal Audit in State Electricity Boards with Special Reference to Andhra Pradesh State Electricity Board", Institute of Public Enterprise, Hyderabad, 1996.
2. Mishra R.K. , "Privatisation in India", in Thine, Ian, and Wetenhal, Roger L (ed), *'Privatisation', International* Institute of Administrative Sciences, Brussels, 1996, pp. 60-70.
3. Reddy, Y.V. , Rao, T.K , Mishra R.K (ed), *Pubic Enterprises : Towards a White Paper*, Institute of Public Enterprise and Booklinks Corporation., Hyderabad,1990, pp. 3-29.
4. Government of India , Report of the Committee on Disinvestment on Shares in Public Sector Enterprises (Rangarajan Committee Report), New Delhi, 1993.
5. Sander. H, *et al.*, "Economic and Corporate Restructuring: Experience and Challenges of the Decade", Lansa Publishing B.V., Leiderdorp, 1998, p. 5.
6. Department of Public Enterprises (Ministry of Industry, Government of India), *Public Enterprises Survey, 1996-97*, Volume 1, New Delhi, pp. 177-183.
7. Government of India, Report of the Committee for Review of Guidelines for Public Sector Enterprises (N. Vittal Committee), New Delhi, 1997.
8. *The Economic Times*, March 15,1999.

Annexure–1

International Comparison of Customer Orientation

	Product Quality[1]	*Product Design*[2]	*On-Time Delivery*[3]	*After-Sales Service*[4]	*Managing Distribution*[5]
India	41.08	34.05	30.27	41.08	52.43
Brazil	52.39	56.62	36.34	39.15	51.83
Thailand	63.00	58.50	57.00	54.00	66.50
South Korea	60.71	48.57	59.29	47.14	57.14
Canada	68.13	58.06	62.19	62.50	66.45
USA	59.67	69.84	62.62	57.70	74.43
Japan	92.68	81.46	93.17	89.76	72.20
Germany	92.50	71.39	88.06	78.61	75.83
France	55.94	66.96	44.64	44.56	66.09
Netherlands	72.89	63.11	69.78	68.44	74.76

Notes:

1. Companies are rated 0 = poor , to 100 = excellent.
2. Includes styling and packaging. Companies are rated 0 = poor, to 100 = excellent.
3. Companies are rated 0 = poor, to 100 = excellent.
4. Companies are rated 0 = poor, to 100 = excellent.
5. Managing channels and distribution. Companies are rated 0 = poor, to 100 = excellent.

Source: Derived from tables in factor III, *The World Competitiveness Report 1990,* IMD and Wordl Economic Forum, Lausanne, Switzerland.

Annexure-2

International Comparison of Human Resource Development

	Vocational Training[1]	*Skilled Labour*[2]	*Worker Motivation*[3]	*Labour Flexibility*[4]	*Managerial initiative*[5]	*Management Education*[6]
India	35.68	64.86	42.17	24.86	60.54	66.49
Brazil	36.62	43.43	53.52	54.65	60.56	49.30
Thailand	45.00	47.00	70.00	63.50	70.00	58.50
South Korea	47.14	59.29	57.86	49.63	67.86	47.14
Canada	39.68	49.06	53.75	47.19	61.56	63.75
USA	48.20	53.44	56.39	64.26	73.67	68.85
Japan	78.50	61.94	84.39	67.80	72.20	59.51
Germany	68.89	50.00	68.06	39.72	72.78	56.94
France	51.18	42.90	51.01	28.99	64.64	59.71
Netherlands	53.33	52.44	64.00	36.44	67.11	53.78

Notes:

1. Extent to which on going job training meets the requirements of a competitive economy: 0 = inadequate to 100 = adequate.
2. Ready availbility of quality skilled labour: 0 = not at all , to 100 = a great extent.
3. Willingness to identify with corporate objectives and priorities: 0 = low , to 100 = high.
4. Managers' sense of drive, responsibility and entrepreneurship: 0 = low, to 100 = high.
5. Extent to which institutions adequately prepare executives for needs of business: 0 = not adequately to 100 = adequately.

Source: Derived from the tables in factor V, *The World Competitiveness Report 1990*, IMD and World Economic Forum, Lausanne , Switzerland.

Annexure-3

International Comparison of R&D Focus

	Total expenditure on R&D as % of GDP (1988)	*Business expenditure on R&D as % of total R&D expenditure (1988)*	*Public funding of total R&D ((1988)*[1]	*Patents*[2]	*Search for technology*[3]
India	0.909	13.05	88.07	0.06	50.11
Brazil	0.381	19.80	66.87	0.32	45.45
Thailand	0.342	13.85	69.57	0.02	61.00
South Korea	1.631	29.61	19.00	1.12	53.51
Canada	1.316	55.74	43.00	4.98	51.11
USA	2.658	70.33	45.88	16.72	62.71
Japan	2.852	66.02	21.46	40.52	85.85
Germany	2.791	74.18	37.66	24.42	68.51
France	2.308	59.77	59.39	16.68	63.21
Netherlands	2.321	59.33	41.74	5.14	59.03

Notes:

1. Percent of total funding provided by the State, 1988.
2. Average annual number of patents granted by residents per 1,00,000 inhabitants, 1985-1988.
3. Efficiency of companies in seeking new technologies and commercially exploiting them: 0 = inefficient , to 100 = efficient.

Source: Derived from tables in Factor IX, *The World Competitiveness Report 1990,* IMD and World Economic Forum, Lausanne, Switzerland.

8

Productivity Improvement Strategies for Indian Public Enterprises

— *R.K. Mishra*

Productivity improvement must be a hallmark of public enterprise reforms in India. These enterprises hold key to the turnaround of the Indian economy. A study of the macro economic aggregates point out that these enterprises contribute 15 per cent to the gross domestic product. Forty-five per cent of the total capital stock formation takes place in these enterprises. The activities of these enterprises cover a very wide spectrum of the economic activities of the country. These enterprises have turned out to be dissavers during the last decade. Their financial performance has eroded their capacity to contribute to the savings stock. It is thus clear that any improvement in the productivity of these enterprises will substantially boost the rate of economic growth in the country. The present paper reflects the productivity scenario in public enterprises on the basis of few parameters. Further, the paper suggests a scheme of measures that can provide a fillip to the productivity in public enterprises.

Productivity Scenario in Public Enterprises

The Product scenario in public enterprises can be studied in relation to the following parameters:

(i) *Profitability:* Profit is the end result of all economic activities. Profitability of an enterprises can be studied in relation to the gross margin of capital employed ratio, operating profits to capital employed ratio, net profit to capital employed ratio and dividends to equity ratio.

(ii) *Value added:* Value added is the net addition of economic value, over and above, the resources used in the form of raw materials, supplies, fuel and appreciation. The value added should be adequate to provide for wages, capital creation and formation of resources. The adequacy of value added can be found out by computing, among other things some ratios such as wages to value added and gross value added to sales.

(iii) *Capital productivity:* Capital productivity is the nerve centre for the generation of profits. In financial terms, the capital productivity can be measured by computing turnover of capital employed, measuring profitability of the uses of assets and multiply by products of the two.

(iv) *Output:* The quantum of output is a key determinant for the sales revenue earned. The quantum of output in an enterprise is effected by capacity utilisation, quality of maintenance and training, and management development. The capacity utilisation ratio, the maintenance ratio and the expenditure on training and management development per employee indicate the potential for the improvement in outputs. The research and development provides a crucial breakthrough in improving outputs. The research and development expenses incurred to sales ratio shows the commitment of an enterprise to boost outputs through research and development.

Profitability

Table 8.1 shows that the gross margin ratio was very low for public enterprises. Analysis of the table points out very clearly that between the manufacturing and the service enterprises, the gross margin ratio was higher in the case of service enterprises. In the normal course, the gross margin to sales ratio should be 30%. In the case of public enterprises this norm was never achieved and was nowhere near the mark. However, some enterprises formed an exception which include Oil & Natural Gas Corporation Limited,

Table 8.1
Profitability Profile of Public Enterprises

(Rs. in crore)

S.No.	Details	88-89	89-90	90-91	91-92	92-93	93-94	94-95	96-97	97-98	97-98
1.	No. of operating enterprises	226	233	236	237	239	240	241	239	238	236
2.	Capital employed	67629	84760	102084	117991	140110	159836	162451	173948	201496	223047
3.	Gross Margin	13438	16412	18312	22223	25227	27707	33384	40161	44809	52615
4.	% of gross margin to capital employed	19.9	19.4	17.9	18.8	18.0	17.3	20.6	23.1	22.2	23.6
5.	Depreciation and deferred revenue expenditure	4866	5790	7210	8548	9270	9151	10754	12574	14201	16522
6.	Gross profit	8572	5790	7210	8548	9270	8151	10754	12574	14201	16522
7.	% of Gross Profit of capital employed	12.7	12.5	10.6	11.6	11.4	11.6	13.9	15.8	15.2	16.2
8.	Interest	4167	5329	7601	9673	10881	11901	12862	13966	15403	16714
9.	Pre Tax Profit/Loss	4405	5293	3501	4003	5076	6655	9768	13621	15206	19379
10.	Tax	1411	1504	1229	1647	1805	2110	2581	4047	5214	5654
11.	Net profit/loss	2994	3789	2272	2359	3271	4545	7187	9574	9992	13725
	(a) Profit of profit making enterprises	4917	5751	5394	6079	7384	9768	12070	14763	16109	20267
	(No. of enterprises)	117	131	123	133	131	121	130	132	130	134
	(b) Loss of loss making enterprises	1923	1962	3122	3723	4113	5223	4883	5188	6117	6541
	(No. of enterprises)	106	98	111	102	106	116	109	102	104	100
	(c) No. of enterprises making neither profit nor loss	3	4	2	2	2	3	2	5	2	2
12.	% of net profit to capital employed	4.4	4.5	2.2	2.0	2.3	2.8	4.4	5.5	5.0	6.2
13.	Dividend	353	323	413	687	792	1028	1436	2205	3084	4051
14.	Retained Profit	2641	3466	1859	1668	2480	3517	5751	7369	6908	9675

Source: Public Enterprises Survey, Vol. I, 1997-98: Department of Public Enterprises, Ministry of Industry, Government of India, New Delhi.

Table 8.2
Wages to Value - Added for State Level Public Enterprises in Madhya Pradesh

List of Enterprises	*92-93*	*93-94*	*94-95*	*95-96*	*96-97*
MP Adviasi Vitta Vikas Nigam	–	–	0.008	0.02	0.01
MP State Employees Housing Corporation	37.85	–17.41	1.14	–27.80	0.38
The Provident Investment Co. Ltd.	0.35	0.16	0.12	0.32	0.37
MP Agro Industrial Development Corporation	0.84	0.90	0.87	0.91	0.77
MP Civil Supplies Corporation	0.92	0.74	0.78	0.98	0.59
MP State Fisheries Development Corporation	0.85	0.83	0.61	0.86	1.07
MP State Electronic Development Corporation	0.21	0.40	0.51	0.52	0.31
MP Forest Development Corporation	0.53	0.89	0.76	0.89	0.87
MP Industries Corporation	0.88	–0.99	0.67	0.83	2.53
MP Mining Corporation Ltd.	0.31	0.80	1.11	0.92	0.92
MP Textile Corporation Ltd.	1.64	1.89	7.24	–4.65	59.48
MP Ware Housing Corporation Ltd.	0.60	0.50	0.57	0.21	0.62
MPS Road Transport Corporation	–	–	1.13	1.47	8.23
MP Export Corporation Ltd.	0.27	0.61	0.75	0.46	0.42
MP Hastashilp Vikas Nigam Ltd.	1.02	5.69	0.96	0.99	0.99
MP Laghu Udyog Nigam	0.66	0.66	0.74	0.71	0.76
MP Land Development Corporation	0.72	0.77	0.76	0.84	0.95
MP Textbook Corporation Ltd.	0.17	0.16	0.67	0.23	–
MP State Tourism Development Corporation	0.99	1.45	0.88	0.90	–
MP Beej Evam Farm Vikas	0.27	0.34	0.40	0.47	0.46

Hypen - sign indicates non-applicability/non-furnishing of information.
Source: ADB Report on State Level Public Enterprises in MP (unpublished).

National Thermal Power Corporation Limited, Indian Oil Corporation Limited, Mahanagar Telephone Nigam Limited, Gas Authority of India Limited, Bharat Heavy Electricals Limited, Hindustan Petroleum Corporation Limited, Northern Coalfields Limited and Bharat Petroleum Corporation Limited. Reasons responsible for the low gross margin earned by public enterprises vary from extensive use of raw materials and over manning and wasteful consumption of energy to high incurrence of indirect costs such as carriage outward, lubricants and watch and ward. Many a public enterprises had created excess capacity to provide expansion, curb project costs. However, in the short and medium-term these have resulted in an increased depreciation charge leading to the reduction of final gross margin.

The operation profit to capital employed should be in the vicinity of 20 percentage points. Table 8.1 shows that the pre-tax profit to capital employed ratio was never more than 10 per cent in public enterprises during the period 1988-89 to 1997-98. The reason responsible for this minimal profitability was an excess interest to gross profit ratio was never 3 to 1. In fact, between 1988-89 and 1995-96 these ratios were in the range of 2 to 1. The extensive interest charged points to the faulty capital structure planning in public enterprises. The net profit should be 10 percent of the capital employed. Table 1 points out that the higher level of the net profit to capital employed ratio was achieved in 1997-98 when it was 6.2 percent. The weak tax planning in public enterprises pushed down the ratio of net profits to employed. Among other things, some enterprises would have restructured their capital mix and reopened their income tax returns to obtain the credit which might have boosted their earnings per share.

The dividends declared on equity capital during 1997-98 turned out to more than 6 percent. The dividend declared should be benchmarked with the bank rate, which is presently 9 per cent.

Value Added

The ratio of wages to value added and wages to sales for some state level public enterprises in Madhya Pradesh have been

Table 8.3
Wages to Sales for State Level Public Enterprises in Madhya Pradesh

List of Enterprises	*92-93*	*93-94*	*94-95*	*95-96*	*96-97*
MP Adviasi Vitta Vikas Nigam	–	–	–	0.83	0.13
MP State Employees Housing Corporation	–	–	1.15	2.50	0.36
The Provident Investment Co. Ltd.	0.39	0.68	1.45	1.48	1.76
MP Financial Corporation	9.78	19.67	27.16	13.30	3.53
MP Agro Industrial Development Corporation	–3.42	5.66	–18.71	2.41	2.62
MP Civil Supplies Corporation	0.0008	0.01	0.01	0.01	0.01
MP State Fisheries Development Corporation	0.48	0.35	0.36	0.57	0.76
MP State Electronic Development Corporation	0.37	3.07	8.125	296.8	10037.00
MP Forest Development Corporation	0.21	0.16	0.12	0.15	0.19
MP Industries Corporation	0.26	0.43	0.16	0.18	0.41
MP Mining Corporation Ltd.	0.19	0.29	0.38	0.41	0.36
MP Textile Corporation Ltd.	0.08	0.08	0.09	0.11	0.15
MP Ware Housing Corporation Ltd.	0.39	0.34	0.39	0.41	0.43
MP Export Corporation Ltd.	0.01	0.01	0.01	0.0009	0.01
MP Hastashilp Vikas Nigam Ltd.	0.57	0.58	0.38	0.47	0.70
MP Laghu Udyog Nigam	0.61	0.61	0.62	0.65	0.69
MP Police Housing Corporation	0.94	0.78	0.78	0.59	0.86
MP Land Development Corporation	0.73	0.70	0.79	0.65	0.84
MP Text Book Corporation Ltd.	0.05	0.04	0.09	0.06	0.00
MP Urja Vikas Nigam Ltd.	0.29	0.21	0.34	0.27	0.45
MP Beej Evam Farm Vikas	0.14	0.17	0.19	0.25	0.24

Hypen - sign indicates non-applicability/non-furnishing of information.
Source: ADB report on state level public enterprises in MP (unpublished).

Table 8.4
Percentage of Value Added to Capital Employed of Some Selected Public Enterprises

S.No.	*Name of the Company*	*% of Value added to Capital Employed* 1997-98	1996-97
1.	Ferro Scrap Nigam Ltd.	64.59	69.10
2.	Indian Iron & Steel Co. Ltd.	–238.32	3382.89
3.	Bharath Alluminium Company Ltd.	38.13	39.47
4.	National Mineral Development Corporation Limited	130.40	109.34
5.	Bharath Cooking Coal Ltd.	109.76	115.18
6.	Neyveli Lignite Corp. Ltd.	33.02	29.62
7.	National Hydro Electric Power Corporation Limited	13.50	14.36
8.	National Thermal Power Corp. Ltd.	24.93	20.38
9.	Bharath Petroleum Corp. Ltd.	118.50	102.45
10.	Fertiliser Corp. of India Ltd.	6.80	1.00
11	Bengal Chemicals & Pharmaceuticals Limited	61.46	61.53
12.	Bharath Heavy Electricals Ltd.	99.55	95.93
13.	Bharath Dynamics Ltd.	70.29	50.54
14.	Goa Shipyard Ltd.	47.62	64.71
15.	National Seeds Corp. Ltd.	49.88	61.18
16.	National Textile Corp. Ltd.	–1.40	–10.89
17.	Tyre Corp. of India Ltd.	14.05	23.89
18.	British India Corp. Ltd.	–5.23	–16.95

Source: Public Enterprises Survey 1997-98: Department of Public Enterprises, Ministry of Industry, Government of India, New Delhi - Vol. I, pp. S-66 to S-70.

given in tables 8.2 and 8.3, respectively. Table 8.2 shows that value added, in most of the enterprises, was in the region of 25 to 30 percent pointing out to the presence of excessive labour force. In some of the enterprises the absence of appropriate technology constraint an effective use of labour. In a large number of public enterprises the absence of proper marketing systems resulted in settling down this ratio at lower levels. Table 8.3 examines the relationship between wages and sales. It may be observed that value added formed a small fraction of sales. Disproportionately very high expense on inputs did not permit value added to assume significant size. The story of the state level public enterprises was no different. A study of the state level public enterprises of Madhya Pradesh supports this generalisation.

Capital Productivity

The capital productivity in public enterprises can be seen in Table 8.4. It is clear from the table that the turnover of capital employed did not exceed 1x meaning thereby that one rupee of investment turned out an output of equal amount. In private sector enterprises the turn over of capital employed is more than 3x.

Output

The capacity utilisation of manufacturing / producing enterprises indicating the number of enterprises which achieved more than 75%, between 50% and 75% and below 50% capacity utilisation, for 1997-98 and previous two years is given in Table 8.5.

It is astonishing to see that 58 public enterprises used their capacity below 50%. The number of such enterprises increased from 49 in 1995-1996 to 58 in 1997-1998. Public Enterprises in the Iron and Steel, Minerals and Metals, Coal and Lignite and Chemicals and Pharmaceuticals sectors were mainly responsible for low capacity utilisation. The reasons responsible for low capacity utilisation ranged from absence of diversification product-mix, technology upgradation, export promotion, provision of captive power plants to improved inventory control, periodic performance review, training and human resource development and professionalisation of Board of Directors.

Table 8.5
Capacity Utilisation in Public Enterprises

S.No.		*1997-98*	*1996-97*	*1995-96*
1.	Units which have recorded capacity utilisation more than 75%	118 (56%)	126 (59%)	122 (56%)
2.	Units where capacity utilisation has been between 50% and 75%	37 (17%)	32 (15%)	48 (22%)
3.	Units where capacity utilisation was less than 50%	58 (27%)	56 (26%)	49 (22%)
	Total units under production surveyed	213 (100%)	214 (100%)	219 (100%)

Source: Public Enterprises Survey 1997-98: Department of Public Enterprises, Ministry of Industry.

Table 8.6
Reserach & Development Expenditure to Sales in Public and Private Sector Units

Year	*Research & Development*		*Sales Turnover (Rs. Crore)*		*Research & Development Eexpenditure as % of Sales turnover (%)*	
	Public Sector	*Private Sector*	*Public Sector*	*Private Sector*	*Public Sector*	*Private Sector*
1990-91	414.53	456.46	91278.85	74669.82	0.45	0.61
1991-92	484.39	525.86	103815.32	87818.51	0.47	0.60
1992-93	586.71	649.89	115848.71	101848.33	0.51	0.64

Source: Data collected and compiled by DST.

Table 8.6 shows the ratio of expenses on R & D to sales in public enterprises. Over the years there has been a considerable erosion in this ratio. During 1980's this ratio was about 2.3 per cent of the total sales. But, in 1990's this has declined to less than 1 per cent of total sales. On the contrary, private sector which used to lag behind has overtaken public enterprises. It spends about 3.5 per cent of its turnover on R & D.

Conclusion

In the present era of globalisation, liberalisation, competition and removal of social inequities, public enterprises have to be productive not only for their own growth but also for the growth of the economies to which they belong. This study on productivity in public enterprises based on different parameters reveals that these enterprises need to transform the existing scenario radically to give a satisfactory account of themselves.

9

Memorandum of Understanding in India : A Performance Improvement Tool for Public Enterprises Performance

Dr. P. Geeta

This paper is an attempt to analyse the working of MoU as a performance evaluation tool for public enterprises in India. It has three sections. Section–I deals with the conceptual background for adopting MoU policy in India. Section–II discusses the infrastructure for implementing MoU. Section–III discussed the critical issues in the adoption of the system and observations from the experiences of enterprises with MoU.

Section–I

MoU Policy in India

The public sector in India, which was synonymous with public good in most of the countries, is currently being viewed as overextented and a drain on the nation's economy. As these enterprises are also unable to made profits, which was not a strong motivation when they were set up, the Government of India, already over burdened with other development responsibilities has lately realized that the public enterprises are a responsibility which it cannot fulfil. In the present era of liberalization and privatization there is a widely shared opinion that the public enterprises cannot be considered as organizations seeking only non-commercial purposes. So the performance of public enterprises is being assessed on par with organizations that are engaged purely in commercial activity. This led to the introduction of the system of MoU as a performance evaluation tool for public enterprises.

The Industrial Policy enunciated by the Government of India from time to time highlighted the critical role of the public sector in the country's economy and accordingly the Government provided the necessary policy and financial support for its growth. On 24th July 1991[1] the Government of India announced a 'Statement on Public Sector Policy' which strongly recommends the need for greater thrust on autonomy through MoU systems through which managers would be granted greater autonomy and will be held accountable. It reiterates that the technical expertise on the part of the Government would be upgraded to make the MoU negotiations and implementation more effective. While focussing on major managerial issue, this would also help place matters of day to day administration of public enterprises in their correct perspective.

Policy Measures for Making Public Sectors Efficient

The Arjun Sengupta Committee was set up in 1985 with view to study the need for a scientific evaluation method for assessing the performance of the public enterprises. The committee submitted its recommendation in 1985. The committee suggested that MoU should be introduced as a tool to measure the performance of public enterprises with a prior exercise on what are the enterprises that have to be included.

The Committee recommended the need for introduction of MoU in response to the widely held perception that the public sector enterprises were less efficient due to lack of operational freedom. The other strong reason that supported the introduction of the MoU system was that the public enterprises were unable to perform as they were pulled in different directions by a number of agencies which were responsible for the enterprise functioning under the ministry concerned as an overall supervisor. For example, Finance Ministry controlling the budget, the Planning Commission regulation the project appraisal and the aid-givers like the IMF, World Bank and others influencing the policy decisions. These organizations set conflicting objectives for the enterprises, and pull them in different directions. This leaves the enterprises with a very little scope to take decisions both (financial and managerial) which can improve their performance.

Concern with Regard to MoU Signatory Enterprises

The central issue in public enterprises is autonomy and accountability. What we mean by autonomy in relation to enterprises is that there should be greater freedom of operation, and powers of decision-making in public enterprises. Empowerment is the key to accountability. If the Board of Directors of an enterprise cannot be trusted to manage the undertaking, the whole set up becomes useless. On the other hand to expect some fast rotating administrative officers in the ministry to monitor, guide and redirect operations of the enterprise is a manifestation of authority and not responsibility.

The system of MoU was introduced in 1987-88 with 4 enterprises signing the MoU in that year. It has grown to 108 enterprises in 1998-99. In a period of seven years the percentage of 'excellent' public sector enterprises varied between 24% to 54%. While the aggregate pattern remained the same, there were substantial variations in terms of individual public sector enterprises. For example, of those evaluated, 51% were rated 'excellent' in 1990-91, which came down to 28% in 1992-93. This percentage went up to 41% again in 1993-94 only to show a downward trend of 39% in 1994-95. In the year 1995-96 it was 30% and again it came down to 24% in the year 1997-98. But the fact remains that the demarcation of ratings between 'very good' and 'excellent' could due to marginal variance in points.

There is another way to look at the enterprises, which have signed the MoU, whether their financial performance has been commensurate with their MoU performance. This does not seem to be the case with enterprises like ONGC that was rated 'excellent' in 1993-94 but its profits came down by Rs. 30 crores form the previous year. In contrast, the case of petroleum sector when analyzed shows that all the nine public sector enterprises in the petroleum sector has signed the MoU have shown an increase of 19% in gross margin and percentage of capital employed to turnover went up form 173% in 1993-94 to 223% in 1994-95. This was mainly due to the upward revisions in the administered prices. This is a fact that we tend to overlook that there has been an additional infusion of investment amounting to Rs 1422 crores during the year 1994-95 alone in the sector. But the public sector enterprises in the petroleum sector have not been rated as 'excellent'. Thus the five-point scale on which the performance of the enterprise is evaluated may not always reflect the real performance of the enterprise.

The basic objective of MoU from the point of view of public sector management is to ensure autonomy. For any organization to perform in an atmosphere of freedom and trust is very essential. In the case of public enterprises the element of autonomy is totally absent making it difficult for the managers to think independently and take bold innovative decisions which are advantageous for the company. The reason for the introduction of the system of MoU into the public sector is to ensure that the managers have adequate autonomy at their disposal. This gives them the necessary operational freedom to make decisions, which are bold and useful for the enterprise. With the introduction of the MoU system there is no real or attitudinal change in the public enterprise government interface. The managements are still subjected to frequent questioning, reporting, refernces and approvals in all business decisions of strategic significance.

The need for accountability in public enterprise arises due to the fact that the investment in public enterprises is done from the public funds and they have to live up to the expectation of the public. The situation is full of conflict in the case of public enterprises because the objectives of the enterprises tend to bring in situations where there is very little freedom at all levels for proving to be a successful commercial management . Any mistake done on the part of the individuals is punishable to any extent but at the same time there is no punishment for non-performance. The public enterprise is expected to work at the same efficiency levels as their private counterparts but with a higher accountability for results. The legislature as well as the audit is always concerned not only with the overall performance of the public enterprise but also with the individual decisions. There is a need to balance both the important elements of autonomy and accountability for a successful running enterprise. If the accountability can be secured on trust and faith then there can be a very congenial atmosphere for proper functioning of the enterprise and at the same time there will be no clash with autonomy. On the other hand there cannot be unfettered autonomy given to any enterprise so the right way would be to balance both the aspects of autonomy and accountability for the proper functioning of an enterprise.

After the introduction of the system of MoU there is no real or attitudinal change in the government about the public-sector government relationship, which spells autonomy. The managements are subjected to frequent questioning, reporting and monitoring and of course interference. The fact remains that the attitudinal changes take place only gradually when a system has been existing for some time, while the system of MoU has been operational for almost a decade and very little change has been realized. This brings home the point that the system of MoU to be more effective needs a lot more preparation, orientation, and operationalisation than has been achieved. This can be made possible by taking initiatives prior to signing the MoU. The committee did not make any suggestions that all the enterprises must be made a part of this system, infact this is the first step towards making the system work. An enterprise that is running in losses and cannot be on its own will eventually be unable to fulfil the commitment laid down by the MoU. Such enterprises should not be made to sign MoU.

After major issue here is that MoU exercise should be more transparent, currently the top layer of management only is involved with the drafting, finalizing, negotiating the MoU. The system needs to be made more transparent. The facts and figures in the MoU must percolate down to the workers level.

Public Enterprise Performance Evaluation

Though there are no formal institutionalized mechanism for evaluation the performance of public enterprises, the public enterprises have been assessed through the years. Firstly we have an Annual Public Enterprise Survey brought out in three volumes. The first volume brings out the figures relation to investment, production, the sources, utilization of funds, value added, gross profit or losses, dividends etc. The survey also highlights the top ten profit making enterprises and the top ten loss making enterprises. The survey gets full coverage in the press and forms the basis for comments on the profitability of the public enterprises. The particular document also influences the general public in regard to the public enterprises. The survey is however useful for statistical purposes and for research work. It is not actually a performance evaluation system and cannot be used for the purpose of management audit. There is one serious drawback in this system[2]. The totality of the central public enterprises includes some high performing and a few not so well performing enterprises. With the aggregate figures we tend to generalize that these figures are for the whole corporate entity i.e. the public enterprises, which is not clearly the case. The investment decision in each case is different and should be evaluated to with reference to that particular reason and objective for the particular decision.

Another broad appraisal of the performance of public enterprises is that which is made by the planing commission in the context of formulation of the Five-Year Plans and the Annual Plans. However, the Planning Commission's essential concern is with the availability of resources for financing the projects and plans, and in the context, with the generation of internal resources by the public enterprises, here too the concern is with the figures.

The importance of quarterly review here becomes very important. This system is prevalent in a number of ministries in the country[3]. Many economic ministries, particularly dealing with the industries and public enterprises have constituted a Management Information system. The secretary of the ministry reviews the reports and returns under this system with the chief executive of the public enterprise present at the meeting. This is the type of a managerial review by the ministry.

The public enterprises also come under the scrutiny of the parliamentary committees. There are a number of committees set up by the parliament in order to scrutinize the working of the public enterprises. There are a few areas, which are taken for investigation by the Parliamentary Committees, and the reports are produced. The various methods of ensuring accountability to the parliament are Parliamentary Questions, Half an Hour discussion on matters related to Public Enterprises, discussion and debates on Budgets, discussion on Annual Reports and Accounts, Committee on Public Undertakings. The Committee on Public Undertakings was constituted on the 21st May 1964. Earlier it had 15 members (10 from Lok Sabha and 5 from the Rajya Sabha) but since 1974-75 it has been increased to 22 (15 from Lok Sabha and 7 from the Rajya Sabha).

The issue is if the government being the owner of the enterprise should be a part of the review process. This gives an impression that the government is acting as a super management and it is above all the other stakeholders for the enterprise. There are other options thrown open by the Jha Commission Report while suggesting that the review on public enterprises must be left to the Board of the enterprise concerned. The Jha Commission has suggested that to avoid misconceptions of the relative role of the ministries and the public enterprise management the information system of the ministry should be called Monitoring Information system rather than Management Information system. The reviews of this kind provide immediate material for eventual evaluation by identifying the immediate problems and their solutions. They even influence the perception of the government too on the performance of the public enterprise.

There have been appraisals and reviews of certain activities of a few public enterprises by the Comptroller and Auditor General of India. The CAG review is usually to identify the loopholes in the assessment done with reference to a few issues like capacity utilization, consumption of input etc. The search is to identify the errors, inefficiency, impropriety, procedural lapses, imprudence etc.

Section–II

Operationalisation of MoU at the Enterprise Level

At the enterprise level the management of public enterprise rests with the Board of Directors, the Chief Executive Officer, heads of various departments. This certainly would not exclude all the stakeholders of the public enterprise. The Board of Directors of the enterprise is the intermediaries between the public enterprise and the government.

They are the chief negotiators for the enterprise on all issues as well as carry out the instructions from the government. The MOU signed by the enterprise is also the responsibility of the Board to see that the targets are met or they should be prepared to give justifications for non-performance of the enterprise. The success of the Board depends on how the enterprise has performed on the basis of the MoU.

The MoU targets are first frame-worked by the Directors and the heads of the various departments of the enterprises. Importantly the team comprises of the Finance Department, the Commerce Department, the Management Services Department, Department of Corporate Planning. The guidelines issued by the Department of Public Enterprises forms the basis for it. The targets are fixed internally first and then discussed with the Board of Directors and finalized. The MoU draft is tabled before the Board of the enterprises. The board then decides about the feasibility of the targets and the requirements by the owner are brought to a final shape.

Then the negotiation process starts with the Chief Executive Officer and his team with the Ministry concerned. The targets prepared internally are then discussed at length and a decision is reached regarding the final targets. These targets are the basis for the MoU evaluation at the end of the year. The heads Finance, Management Services, Corporate Planning, Commerce etc. are all an important of the negotiation process for target setting.

The system of performance evaluation in public enterprises has been prevalent from a long time though there has not been a institutionalized scheme for evaluating the enterprises. The need for introducing a systematic evaluation method for the enterprises was felt and was conceived by the Arjun Sengupta Committee recommendations. The report stressed the need for a comprehensive evaluation package for the public enterprises. The present system of performance evaluation involves the public enterprises to enter into an agreement with the Government of India in the beginning of every financial year by signing the MoU. The MoU is a comprehensive document, which contains the

(1) Mission of the enterprise

(2) The Corporate Objectives

(3) The Performance Criteria

(4) The Values attached to the indicators

(5) An Evaluation Process

(6) Scoring.

The targets are set at the beginning of the year and based on the targets, evaluation is carried out at the end of the year. An assessment is made if the enterprises have been able to achieve the targets set for them and grading based on the performances are given to each of the enterprises.

Need for Scientific Approach

The public enterprises in India needed the induction of scientific assessment methodology for assessing their performance. There was no account of the losses as well as the profits they were making. Generally there was no way to comprehensively judge the performance of the public enterprises. As they were set up with a view of social justice yet they needed to be doing financially well. This made the MoU system a very necessary tool for the evaluation of the performance of public enterprises.

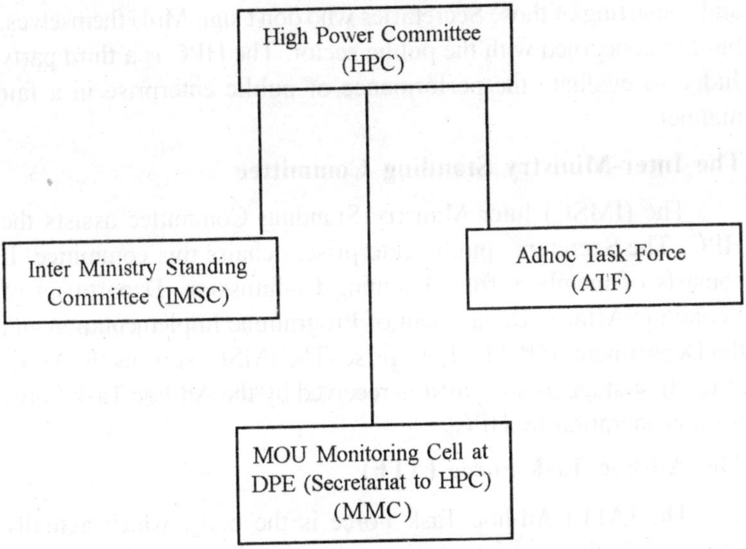

Section–III

Infrastructure for MOU in India

The MoU system in India originated as a result of the Arjun Sengupta Committee report in 1985. The enterprises adopted the system in the year 1987-88. Initially the system was introduced on the French lines. It was virtually a Performance Information System. The contents of the contract were only useful for the owner of the enterprise, as they had no mission, objectives or goals well defined in them. Later in the year 1989-90 the contractual system was rebuilt on the Korean lines. The contracts started having well defined mission, objectives and goals. It also very clearly decided about the performance criteria, gave appropriate weightage to them and finally evaluated them on a five point rating scale. Design and implementation of the MoU system for the Central Public Enterprises in India is the responsibility of the Department of Public Enterprises in the Ministry of Industry.

High Power Committee

At the apex of the framework is the High Power Committee (HPC). It is the overall in charge, chaired by the Cabinet Secretary and consisting of those Secretaries who don't sign MoU themselves, but are concerned with the public sector. The HPC is a third party Judge to evaluate the performance of public enterprise in a fair manner.

The Inter-Ministry Standing Committee

The (IMSC) Inter Ministry Standing Committee assists the HPC. The Secretary (public enterprises) chairs this committee. It consists of members from Planning Commission, Department of Economic Affairs, Department of Programme Implementation and the Department of Public Enterprise. The IMSC, screens the MoU, at the first stage as soon as it is received by the Ad-hoc Task Force for consideration by HPC.

The Ad-hoc Task Force (ATF)

The (ATF) Ad-hoc Task Force is the body, which actually performs all the negotiations on targets and other important clauses. It consists of eminent management expects, ex-chief executives, chartered accountants, academicians and economist. It is a body of experts who bring in high level of expertise and credibility to the whole system of MoU.

MoU - Monitoring Call (MMC)

The MoU monitoring cell is the nucleus of the whole contracting system. It is located at the department of public enterprise. All coordinating activities relating to the design, drafting, finalization, this cell does monitoring and evaluation of the MoUs.

There are a number of factors that have come to light about the working of this system during the study. There are a few points that have been discussed below:

(i) The High Power Committee (HPC), at the apex provides commitment at the higher level.

(ii) The Ad-hoc Task Force, as a technical third party judge gives objectivity to the MoU evaluation.

(iii) The presence of professionals and experts as members of ATF add to the professionalism to the evaluation system.

(iv) The number of enterprises covered by MoU has come up to 109 in 97-98 which makes the procedure highly routinized. There is not enough time to concentrate on issues of concern.

(v) The absence of political commitment is seen as giving negative impact to the MoU system.

(vi) Lack of proper incentive system at different levels of hierarchy is an important factor, which has not given a boost to the MoU system.

Section–III

Critical Issues in the Adoption of the System

The issue of internalization was discussed in detail in a survey of 110 MoU signing enterprises. The enterprises were asked to look into the MoU internalization in their organization. There are a number of issues at the enterprise level that have to be understood for having a complete picture of the system:[2]

1. The level of transparency in the enterprise about the MOU process. Is it restricted to the top management only or is shared with senior, middle level executives.
2. What are the organizational arrangements at the enterprise level? Weather a separate cell is created in the enterprise like the MoU cell at the Department of Public Enterprise.
3. Wheather MoU is linked with the corporate plan of the enterprise.
4. Wheather MoU is linked to the restructuring plan.
5. Wheather the enterprise has an internal monitoring system to check weather performance is per the MoU criteria.
6. Linkages with budgetary control system and other performance assurance systems. Weather MoU targets are synonymous with budgets, etc. to avoid multiplicity of performance monitoring system.
7. Linkages with divisional performance measurement system: weather performance measurement methods in the MoU and the divisional performance system are same.

8. Weather MoU signing is used as an opportunity for changing the organizational strategies in the wake of liberalization.
9. Internal incentive scheme to boost performance.
10. Intangible Vs tangible performance criteria.
11. International standards for internal performance evaluation.
12. Experience with respect to the number of reports to be sent to the administrative ministry as distinct from reports to other governmental agencies. Weather the number by chance has increased.

Impact of the System of MoU

The system of MoU has been in vogue for more than a decade. It seems to have a marginal impact on the public enterprise performance. It has not been able to provide autonomy to the enterprises, both financial and managerial, which was one of the major objectives for the introduction of the system. The issue of autonomy has still not been set in place and the issue of accountability still remains dicey.

The Tables 9.1 and 9.2 below clearly highlight that in the initial years of introducing the contractual system in the public enterprises there was a gradual improvement in the performance of the public enterprises. It is noticed that after a brief period i.e. 2-3 years of the introduction of the system a downward slide is marked which continues in most of the enterprises. It has been observed even in the case studies that there was a positive trend seen in the performance of the enterprises right at the beginning i.e. in 1991-92 when the system of MoU was introduced into the Public enterprises. Gradually there is a slide down in the performance around 1994-95 and again the enterprises are showing an upward trend in their performance.

The general survey that was conducted on the 109 enterprises signing MoU also brought out the fact that the enterprises were a bit enthusiastic about the system in the beginning when it was introduced in 1991-92. The system of MoU has hardly enhanced the powers to the enterprises, and has enhanced accountability. The system has left the enterprises disillusioned.

Table 9.1
MoU Entered by CPES between 1988-89 and 1997-98

Particulars	*88-89*	*89-90*	*90-91*	*91-92*	*92-93*	*93-94*	*94-95*	*95-96*	*96-97*	*97-98*
No. of entrep-rises entered MOU	11*	18	23	71	98	101	99	104	110	109
Graded										
Excellent		9	14	25	34	44	44	52	46	45
Very Good		3	5	21	35	30	28	31	27	25
Good		5	-	9	16	17	7	7	19	13
Fair		-	-	3	10	7	8	12	11	14
Poor		-	1	-	2	1	2	2	7	11
Not Graded										
		1	-	13	1	4	10	0	0	0

* In 1988-89, the MOU were negotiated on the basis of parameters such as gross sales, gross margin,etc.
The system of composite score evaluation came into operation from 1989-90.

Source: Department of Public Enterprises, Government of India, New Delhi, Annual Survey on Public Enterprises, Vol. 1, for the years 1987-88 to 1994-95.

Table 9.2
Performance Status in Terms of MoU Ratings between 1989-90 and 1996-97

Performace Status	*Years*						
	1990-91	*1991-92*	*1992-93*	*1993-94*	*1994-95*	*1995-96*	*1996-97*
Down	4	3	10	21	17	14	24
Up	1	1	8	22	21	17	16
Same	7	10	31	46	41	44	49

Source: Public Enterprises Survey, Vol. 1, 1989-90 to 1993-94, Department of Public Enterprise, Government of India.

The table 9.1 shows that the number of enterprises that signed MoU in the year 1988-89 were only 11 which went up to 109 in the year 1997-98. There is a trend that is visible by the table that the enterprises that have ben graded as excellent in the year 1989-90 were 9, which rose up to 45 in the year 1997-98. In the similar way the enterprises that had been graded as very good were 3 in the year 1989-90 which rose up to 25 in the year 1997-98. The enterprises that were graded good too went up from 5 in the year 1989-90 to 13 in the year 1997-98. The enterprises that were graded poor and fair too went up in numbers from 0 and 1 respectively in the year 1989-90 to 14 and 11 in the year 1997-98.

As per the table 9.2 number of enterprises that have shown a downward slide in their performance ratings in the year 1990-91 remain 4 and while the number again rose to 24 in the year 1996-97. The number of enterprises that have shown an upward performance trend in the year 1990-91 were 1, which went up to 16 in the year 1996-97. The number of enterprises that showed no change in their performance remain 7 in the year 1990-91 and 49 in the year 1996-97 respectively.

Internalization Experience of Enterprises with MoU

The study shows that out of the 110 enterprises signing MoU, only in a few of them the system has not percolated down to

The essential points that are brought out from the survey are;

1. The system has brought about greater fiscal discipline among the MoU signing enterprises by assigning 60% weight to financial performance. It has ensured that no Public sector enterprise can be rated excellent unless it exceeds its budgeted targets for financial performance.

2. Since the focus, under the MoU system, has shifted to achievement of results, Ministries have begun to withdraw from their tendency to control by procedures. MoU has thus increased the operational autonomy of the enterprise.

3. Delegating more financial and administrative powers to the MoU signing public enterprises has also increased operational autonomy of the enterprises.

4. By laying stress on marketing effort and comparing with the private sector enterprises, MoU are keeping public sector enterprises to face competition.

5. MoU has led to greater coordination among the ministries as well as between the PSE's and the ministries. The High Power Committee on MoU, which consists of Secretaries of Planning, Financing, Expenditure and Program Implementation, ensures that all contradictions are removed or minimized. Similarly the Ad-hoc-Task Force (ATF) on MoU during its meeting with the PSE's is able to highlight the issue requiring coordination among the PSE's and the Ministries.

6. The Quarterly Performance Review (QPR) meeting have become more focussed since the introduction of MoU's Discussion is confined to overall achievement as outlined in the MoUs. This has led to higher quality of debate about PSE's performance.

7. By making a distinction between enterprise performance and managerial performance, MoU's will have improved the quality of debate and made the judgement on PSE Management

References

1. *Public Enterprise Survey*, Government of India, 1997-98.

2. Vithal, M.P. *Internalization of MoU by Public Enterprises: A Management Control Approach to Performance Improvement.*

10

Financial Autonomy and Accountability of Public Enterprises

— R.K.Mishra

This paper attempts to explain the concept of financial autonomy and financial accountability in Public Enterprises (PEs), describe various tiers of financial autonomy and financial accountability in PEs, and discuss suggestions for ensuring improved autonomy and accountability of PEs. The extent of Financial autonomy and accountability has been at the heart of discussions about improving the performance of PEs. There have been conflicting views about the right mid of financial autonomy and accountability, which can ensure an efficient and effective performance from these enterprises. It goes without saying that there is no well-defined formula available in this respect, which can be suggested to the principals (government) and the agents (PEs). What is required is to inculcate awareness about striking the golden mean between the financial accountability and the financial control among those who hold the reins of the government and PEs in their hands. The right mix will emerge as a result of the mutual understanding of the needs on the part of the principals and agents and the restraints that both will impose on each other to fined an agreed solution to the problem.

Concept of Financial Autonomy and Accountability in PEs

The financial autonomy to PEs means empowering them to take decisions on their own in the areas of investment management, financing of investments and checking upon the financial performance based on the sound business principles and the wisdom of the financial administrators. In so far as investments are concerned, other things remaining the same, PEs should have a free go in identifying the projects, preparing the feasibility and detailed project reports, appraising the projects, making investment choices, and implementing and monitoring them.

They should also be free to decide the optimal level of investments in the various items of Inventory book debts and floating stock of cash. By the same principle they should be free to peg the level of current liabilities to any proportion of the current assets. The financial decisions in the normal run may be made by these enterprises as guided by the cost of capital. They should possess the freedom to choose among the various debt-equity propositions. They should be at their liberty to select bankers, financial institutions and the channels of money and capital markets for financing their working fund requirements. Subject to the social constraints imposed on them by the government, these enterprises should be vested with the autonomy to develop their own costing and pricing systems, norms of profitability and monitoring mechanism to ensure the desired financial status alike any business firm in the private sector.

Prof. V.V. Ramanadham in his treatise entitled "The Control of PEs in India" discusses the concept of financial accountability. Primarily it implies the accountability of PEs to parliament in financial matters. So expressed, it is part of the general problem of amenability of PEs to parliamentary control and calls for a compromise between the democratic rights of parliament and the autonomy of the enterprises. The other aspect of financial accountability is that the maximum good results ought to be secured from the PEs. So expressed, it borders on the concept of efficiency in financial terms. The maximisation is not tantamount to an insistence on the highest possible profit from every public enterprise. The concept suggests that, subject to any set criterion of profit and social benefit, the enterprise ought to record the best possible results.

Tiers of Financial Autonomy and Accountability in PEs

Financial autonomy is a phenomenon external to the organisation. In other words, it flows from the environment governing the functioning of PEs . Thus there are Six tiers of financial autonomy. These include the parliament, the government, the Comptroller and Auditor General (CAG) of India, the Courts of Law, the mass media and the common man. All these six institutions can have an explicit policy about the financial autonomy they may like to provide to PEs in order to enable them to operate efficiently and effectively. As the enterprises under discussion are both 'public' and 'enterprise', these institutions cannot be over jealous in controlling each and every aspect of financial business of PEs. The respect for the corporate status of these enterprises will have to be maintained by these institutions. While saying so we do not deny the need for exercising checks and balances on the financial decision-making in these enterprises. What we are trying to put forward is the argument that these institutions should be selective in exercising the financial controls on PEs. PEs may enjoy autonomy in the day-to-day financial decision making which in its ambit may include matters such as normal purchases, cost allocations, evolving suitable price structures, selection of suitable sources and mix of finance, installation and operation of the financial information systems, and preparation and finalisation of accounts, etc. On the reverse, the six institutions may intervene in the policy aspects of the financial decision-making. For instance, if the parliament so desires it may discuss the financial performance, financial position, pricing, financial aspects of foreign collaborations and the position of internal financing in PEs, etc. The government may reserve the right to approve the appointments of executives drawing salaries above certain levels and issue directives to PEs to provide certain services of particular prices, even if they are not economical. The CAG can give directions to PEs to follow a specific format for the presentation of their accounts and disclosure of the financial information. The various courts of law may direct PEs to alter their financial decisions if the fundamental rights of the citizens are affected, in their opinion contrary to what contained in Articles 12 and 14 of the India Constitution. The mass media and the various publics may resent against certain financial decisions by PEs and as a result they may have to reconsider the matter. Such decisions may include matters relating to pricing, and selection of suppliers of plant and materials, which may cause the public dissent.

Major Accounting Decisions: There are four tiers of financial accountability. These include: financial accountability. These include: arise in the fields of depreciation, tender procedures, stores valuation and replacements.

Matters of Internal Organisation: These include internal audit, procedures for ordering materials, the delegation of powers, watch and ward supervision over the financial transaction, penal provisions on staff misbehavior etc. are examples of matters which may based up lift to properly evolved system of internal organisation within the enterprise itself.

Broad Financial Policies: These are a fundamental aspect of financial accountability. They require plans between a board's own plans and the socio-economic aims set by the parliament. These may include the matters pertaining to the illustrations of self-financing, the outlines of capital expansion programmes and the extent of dividend reputation to foreign funds or the consultancy fees.

National Policies: PEs may express their accountability to the various institutions in respect of the financial results, productivity and growth. The memorandum of understanding (MOU) is emerging as an important instrumentality whereby PEs are required to spell

The Methods of Ensuring Financial Autonomy and Accountability in PEs

To ensure financial autonomy both the external and internal methods have been resorted to. Externally the government prescribes the financial freedom to PEs in regard to several aspects in their articles of association. The limits for investment, commercial borrowings, working capital borrowings, and salaries offered to employees and powers of recruitment, etc., are specified in the articles of association. The provisions regarding business budgeting, costing and pricing etc., are also contained therein. The government indicates the autonomy to PEs in respect of pricing, investment and profitability in the MOU. In the articles of association as well as the enabling acts under which public corporations have been set up the government impose a self-restraint on itself to interfere in the day to day working of PEs including matters pertaining to the financial functioning. Internally PEs ensure autonomy at the different levels of functioning by enforcing delegation and decentralisation of financial powers. In many a PE, there is a healthy tradition to hold group meetings which are also known as communication meetings. In these meetings the departmental heads are the invitees. The workers' representatives are also invited. The problems are discussed and decisions are taken then and there. These meeting deal with the decisions regarding procurement, plant acquisition, investment of funds and acceptance of tender. This instrument provides a great deal of financial autonomy to the executives and work force.

The methods of ensuring financial accountability may be divided broadly into two categories: organisational methods and the external methods. The former may take the shape of arrangements which may enable a PE to give a good financial account of itself. The external means may be a sequel to the autonomous organisation of a PE, created for ensuring that the managers, to whom it does not belong, behave responsibly vis-a-vis the parliament.

The organisational means of financial accountability are as follows:

(b) Clear financial procedures

(c) Efficient internal audit

(d) Commercial audit by private auditors

(e) Proper internal organisation of the enterprise, based on optimal criteria and decentralisation

(f) Provision of a really autonomous top board

(g) Appointment by the government, or under governmental approval, of a Financial Adviser to the enterprise

(h) Governmental control through board composition

(i) Reservation of certain financial matters for government decision, under the Articles of Association or under the Act governing a public enterprise

(j) Audit by the CAG.

Status of Financial Autonomy and Accountability in PEs

Though financial autonomy is a much talked about phenomenon, there are plenty of bindings on PEs imposed by the diktates from the enabling legislations, parliament and the administrative ministry. The DVC Act makes it obligatory on the Damodar Valley Corporation to report on 10 financial matters, obtain approval on 15 financial matters and receive the directions from the Minister on 5 financial matters. As discussed earlier in the guise of serving the public interest, a minister can always issue a formal directive to PEs. There have been cases of frequent lunch-table directives to PEs by the government. One of the reasons as to why PEs have missed linking costs with prices can be found in the undue interference by the government in their working. The un-optimal debt-equity ratios and the un-suitable financing mix is also the government's gift to these enterprises. The guidelines issued by the Department of Public Enterprise (then Bureau of Public Enterprises) corroborate our assertion. There are more than 200 guidelines on financial matters. These guidelines range from the rate of interest which PEs should pay on their borrowings to the dividend pay-out ratio which they must maintain while deciding about the retention of profits. In fact, PE managers, annoyed by these guidelines, started comparing the Bureau of Public Enterprises with the fifth wheel in the coach. Parliament directly exercises control inas much as its prior approval is required for certain investments in PEs and reports are to be submitted to it in certain other cases, as shown below. This however, applies only to new services, that is, for new activities, taken up for the first time. Further, such approvals are only financial and not administrative. The parliament is not in session, the money may, in case of emergency be provided out of the contingency fund and the sanction of parliament is obtained at a later date.

The parliamentary approvals on the financial matters have to be taken as below:

(i) *Approval of Parliament*: Limits beyond which prior approval is needed, even if there is a budget provision:

(a) Setting up of any new government company, splitting of an existing company, amalgamation of two or more government companies, taking up of new activity by an existing government company or a department undertaking.

Paid-up Capital	*Limit*
Upto Rs. 1 crore	Rs. 20 lakhs or more
Above Rs. 1 crore and upto 25 crores	Rs. 2 crores or more
Above Rs. 25 crores and upto 100 crores	Rs. 10 crores or more
Above Rs. 100 crores	Rs. 15 crores or more

(b) Additional investment in an existing departmental undertaking beyond Rs. 1 crore.

(c) Additional investment in or loans to an existing government company. The limits would depend up on the existing paid-up capital of the company, and/or as follows:

The above limits cover both the loans and capital investments taken together. It there is no budget provision, prior approval of parliament is necessary in the case of loans exceeding Rs. 20 lakhs to an existing government company.

Paid-up Capital	*Limit*
Upto Rs. 1 crore	Rs. 10 lakhs and above, but below Rs. 20 lakhs
Above Rs. 1 crore and upto 25 crores	Rs. 1 crores and above, but below Rs. 2 crores
Above Rs. 25 crores and upto 100 crores	Rs. 5 crores and above, but below Rs. 10 crores
Above Rs. 100 crores	Rs. 7.50 crores and above, but below Rs. 15 crores

(ii) *Reporting to parliament*: Limits beyond which report to parliament is necessary along with the ensuing batch of supplementary demands for grants:

(a) Additional investment (both loan and equity taken together) to an existing public undertaking/government company, as per the following limits:

(b) All additional investments in an existing departmental undertaking of Rs. 50 lakhs and above, but below Rs. 1 crore.

(c) Short-term (working capital) loans not exceeding one year as per the limits prescribed in (i)–(c) above.

In respect of the following, PEs need prior approval of the government:

(i) Capital expenditure where the detailed project-report has been approved by the government, if the variations in the approved estimates are more than 10 per cent.

Investment in the enterprise	*Amount beyond which capital expenditure would need approval*
Rs.	*Rs.*
100 crores or more	1 crore
Between 50 crores and 100 crores	50 lakhs
Between 20 crores and 50 crores	40 lakhs
Between 5 crores and 20 crores	20 lakhs
Below 5 crores	15 lakhs

(ii) Capital expenditure on works taken up in advance of the preparation of detailed project reports or otherwise as individual works beyond the prescribed limits. The limits are laid down with reference to total capital investment in an enterprise as given below:

(iii) Appointments of persons who have attained the age of 58 years, if appointed in the scale of Rs. 2500-3000 and above. (It may be noted that a PE can offer any salary to a person below 58 years, without reference to the government.)

(iv) Formation of a subsidiary company.

(v) Making of rules governing the conditions of service of the employees' provident fund and to create reserves and special funds.

(vi) Giving an employee a commission on the profits of the business of the enterprise.

(vii) The plans, of development and capital budget of the enterprise, and also the revenue budget, if there is an element of deficit in it, which is proposed to be met by the government.

(viii) Agreements involving foreign collaborations.

(ix) Borrowings, investments, and distribution of profits.

The above provisions do not apply uniformly in all cases.

The systems and procedures derived to ensure the financial accountability in PEs are very detailed and elaborate. The parliament debates the financial issues relating to PEs at the time of the budget discussions and the question hour. Further, to look into the financial performance of PEs and to check upon their commercial and business prudence, the Committee on Public Undertakings (COPU) a standing committee on PEs set up by the parliament, also helps it on a continuing basis to develop a proper perspective in relation to the financial matters of these enterprises. The COPU has, in Its life span of the last 28 years, submitted to the parliament about 600 reports. It has also carried out a number of horizontal studies. A couple of these studies have been on financial aspects the prominent which are the reports entitled "Financial Management in PEs", and "Galloping expenditure on foreign travels in PEs" etc. The government controls on PEs make the financial accountability a very painful task. The reports and returns submitted on financial aspects are monthly, quarterly and annual in nature. If these enterprises incur losses, then they have to get even their revenue budget approved by the administrative ministry. The CAG carries out not only financial but also efficiency and propriety audits for these enterprises. The annual reports place these enterprises into a disadvantageous position vis-a-vis their counterparts in the private sector on account of time over runs and poor quality of financial disclosure.

Problems Pertaining to Financial Autonomy and Accountability in PEs

The financial autonomy and accountability of PEs occupy an important place in a democratic country such as ours. However, as the things stand, these are treated as two separate facets of the personality of PEs and consequently a friction arises between the government and PEs on the issues relating to autonomy and accountability. Mr. V. Krishna Murthy, the former chief executive of the Steel Authority of India, had observed that there is a need to find the right balance between the financial autonomy and financial accountability. He likened them with the two sides of the same coin. He suggested getting out of this flip-floppy on financial autonomy and financial accountability and preparing the ground for the evaluation of better managerial practices. An important problem in this context is the government's resistance on getting matters referred to it on the various financial issues and the aversion of PEs to disclose the requisite financial information to their principals. Both the government and PEs are responsible for this sad state of affairs. Whereas the government continues to treat these enterprises as its extensions, PEs do not make involved efforts to come out of the gravitational pull of the government . The parliament, the administrative ministry, the CAG and the Courts treat themselves as the trustees of public funds are prompted, therefore, to impose extensive financial controls on these enterprises. They do not want to take any risk with the public money, but prefer safety and security. The need of the hour is to treat PEs a more like any other commercial organisation in order to achieve the maximum public good.

Suggestions for Ensuring Improved Autonomy and Accountability of PEs

A number of suggestions can be offered to ensure improved financial autonomy and accountability in PEs. To begin with, these enterprises should be commercialised. This will enable PEs to charge economic rates of the goods and services provided to their users. This will result into the generation of adequate internal resources and consequent reduction of financial support from the government to fund their operation and expansion needs. In turn, the government control on financial matters will decline drastically. The corporatisation of these enterprises can be another suggestion to tackle the problem of autonomy and accountability. This will transform the systems, structure and strategy of PEs and resolve many thormy problems afflicting the financial autonomy and accountability. A large number of PEs and resolve many thormy problem afflicting the financial autonomy and accountability. A large number of PEs have been complaining about lack of autonomy to them as they do not have adequate powers to procure the requisite amount of materials, stores and supplies etc. On the reverse, the government is of the view that the inventories in these enterprises should be rigorously controlled, as there is a heavy over-investment in this component of assets in PEs. The government's suspicion cannot be questioned, as many a PE do not have materials management manual. The absence of such a manual has encourage them to procure materials disproportionate to their needs. The CAG in his various audit repots has commented upon the non-preparation of the budget, cost, internal audit, R & D and capital expenditure manuals. Many PEs do not have even the budget manual. The enhanced delegation and decentralisation of financial powers within PEs is a must. In order to achieve this objective well-defined structures must be developed. The boards of management in PEs should specify the financial powers vested in each functionary. Similarly, the various executives in PEs should be encouraged to delegate financial powers to their junior colleagues. The government, on its part, should resist the tendency of biting more than what it can chew. Instead of putting limits on investments, expenditure, borrowings, etc. it may better issue some suggestive guidelines. In case a PE exceeds the suggested ceiling, it may be required at the best of report the matter to the government. The principle of management no by exception can come in handy here. The government should intervene only in such cases where it is necessary to do so as governed largely by the in the order of public interest.

PEs should formulate very clearly these financial strategies and goals, which should be both unambiguous and quantifiable. For instance, PEs should very clearly specify that they propose to earn a 20 per cent rate of return on their capital employed, declare 10 per cent dividend on their equity, finance 50 per cent to their expansion programme through internal generation of resources and approach the capital market to finance rest of their expansion needs. This clarity in the financial objectives will enable PEs to acquire the necessary financial autonomy from the government, on the one hand, and lead to self-imposed controls on the other, which will do away with the need of clamping financial controls on them by the government. These must be a sincere application of the MBO to attain financial objective.

It is desirable to eliminate the multiple audits, in PEs, which are not only unproductive but also uncalled for in view of the fact that the counterparts of PEs in the private sector are not required to follow such a binding. The efficiency and propriety audits are merely philosophies. Thus there is no need to carry out such audits in the case of PEs. The audit approach needs to undergo a change in order to yield the desired results. The auditors must be made conversant with the operations and philosophy of PEs and the environment gravitating their day-to-day working.

The annual reports can serve, as an important medium to satisfy autonomy and accountability needs. They can be a good instrument to win greater autonomy for PEs and fulfil, at the same time, the control needs of the parliament, CAG, Courts and the various publics. An analysis of the annual reports of PEs shows that they are not brought out in time. The time lag in their finalisation and presentation to the parliament ranges from one year to ten years. Secondly in many cases they are either sketchy or they do not provide important information relating to the trends in output, productivity, prices, profitability, comparative performance and the economies effected. Necessary steps must be taken to improve the practices pertaining to the preparation and presentation of the annual reports by PEs.

The High Courts and the Supreme Court have accepted many writ petitions on PEs regarding the financial matters. Some of these relate to the procurement of materials and payment of pension etc. Articles 12 and 14 of the Indian Constitution have been extended to even PEs whereby these enterprises have been considered as State. As discussed earlier, PEs contain not only 'public' but the 'enterprise' element. Thus there is a need to introduce an amendment in the

Indian Constitution to take PEs out of the purview of Articles 12 and 14.

Financial Autonomy and Accountability of PEs: Recent Trends

There is no denying the fact that the government is convinced about providing more autonomy to PEs and reducing the wide-randing financial, controls on them. The approach outlined in the budget speeches of the Finance Minister in 1991-92 and 1992-1993, the observations made in the economic survey of 1991-92 and the letter on development policy sent by the Finance Minister to the World Bank President describes the various steps the government proposes to take in this regard.

The government proposes to classify PEs as competitive and noncompetitive units. About 140 units at the central level have been identified as competitive PEs. These enterprises will be guided by the market forces i their financial matters. The government will refrain from issuing guidelines or directives in the financial matters to these enterprises. They will be free to decide their financing, pricing and costing policies. They will be at their liberty to develop suitable systems and structures to achieve the overall financial objectives. These enterprises being non-core in nature will not receive any budgetary support. They will have to finance of their needs through the internal generation of resources and mobilisation of money from capital markets. There will be disinvestments of equity in these enterprise to the extent of 20 per cent. The member of the government nominees on the board of directors of PEs will be reduced 'one'.

The government is reviewing the guidelines issued on financial matters to PEs. There is every possibility that most of these guidelines will either be scraped or reformulated in order to provide a free go of PEs in financial matters. There is a possibility that the government may withdraw the multiple audits on PEs. As a matter of fact it was only in 1950s that such an audit was imposed on PEs at the initiative of the CAG.

The government is taking appropriate steps to improve the quality of financial reporting in PEs through their annual reports. The various state governments in the country are giving a top priority to streamline the preparation of annual accounts and annual reports in the SLPEs.

An adequate financial autonomy is a necessary condition for the successful working of PEs. This autonomy should not only flow from the government but it should further percolate from top down to the bottom at the different levels in PEs. The financial controls are an important phenomenon in a democratic set up. These controls should, however, be not regressive. The state of art of the financial autonomy and financial accountability pin-points that the delicate balance between the two has been lost. Whereas there is an over emphasis on financial accountability, PEs have failed in using whatever little leverage has been provided to them in respect of the financial autonomy. The Parliament, the Government, the CAG and the various publics need to exercise self-restraint on imposing too many financial controls on PEs. PEs on their part should perform better.

11

Financial Administration of Public Enterprises

— R.K.Mishra

This paper attempts to state the importance of financial administration in public enterprises (PEs); discuss the mechanics of financial administration in PEs; highlight the financial policy for PEs; and explain the new initiatives in the field of financial administration in PEs. Financial administration is the key functional area in the management of PEs. The financial administrators of PEs have to interact continuously with the other operating administrators to achieve the financial objectives. Finance is a service function and, therefore, the counterparts of financial administrators in other operating departments approach them to receive the requisite decisional inputs to execute their responsibilities. In all the stages of operations, finance function occupies the place of primacy. Under gestation, finance is required for the implementation of projects. In the normal run of the business, finance provides capital for meeting the day-to-day needs i.e., working capital. In expansion, finance provides resources both for current operations and execution of new projects.

Meaning and Definition of Financial Administration in PEs

Financial administration in PEs has been defined variously. According to one school of thought, financial administration in PEs means raising the funds to fulfil the financing needs. This definition limits the scope of financial administration to the methods and instruments of raising finance. It presents the conventional view of financial administration in PEs. Today, financial administration goes far beyond the task of raising finance and deciding about the mix of financial instruments. According to another view, financial administration in PEs deals with the management of cash. This definition implies that all such activities, which affect the cash flow in PEs, can be considered as financial administration.

This is a very broad definition of financial administration as there cannot be many activities, which do not influence the cash flow in PEs, and as such it lacks operational validity. Some experts conceptualise financial administration in PEs as that bunch of activities, which deal with raising of finance, its allocation among different uses and checking upon their financial performance. This definition possesses conceptual clarity and also combines operational validity.

View Points of Financial Administration in PEs

As noted earlier, financial administration is one of the major functions in PEs. It has to frequently interface with the other business functions. A healthy interaction between fiance and non-finance administrators is principal requisite for a successful functioning of PEs. The situation obtaining in this regard shows scant respect for financial administrators by other functionaries in PEs and vice-versa. Despite the usefulness of financial input in operating decisions, the operating administrators refrain from Interacting with the financial administrators. There is a popular belief that finance functions is disliked by the various functionaries in PEs. However, a study on the audit practices carried out by the Institute of Public Enterprises reveals that about 85 per cent of functionaries at all the level and in the different age groups preferred the continuation of audit. The financial administrators have brought this important function to disrepute because they try to control the performance of their counterparts of means and in the operating departments more in terms procedures that ends. In terms of the help provided to the non-finance executives, the financial administrators are found mostly indifferent. The ideal state is one of providing active help. The exercise of the preparation and execution of budgets can be cited as a case in point. The budget should not be reduced to a game of numbers by financial administrators. It should be transformed into an exercise that may enlist the support and cooperation of all functionaries in PEs. On the part of the non-finance functionaries, they will do well to inculcate a positive approach to finance function and overcome the inertia of consulting the financial administrators as and when required from time to time.

Financial Policy of PEs

The financial policy of PEs is designed to achieve an optimal output at the lowest cost. It further aims to arrange to provide the financial inputs in a manner that may contribute to smooth functioning of PEs. In the effort to achieve this end, financial administration have to execute the following functions:

Acquisition of Long-Term Sources of Funds

The financial administrator has a dual responsibility with regard to the acquisition of funds. He advises on the choice of appropriate sources of funds and then takes steps to procure the funds from the chosen sources. The funds employed in the enterprise may be classified into two groups, long-term funds and short-term funds. The long-term sources are further classified as debt and equity. Successful enterprises seek debt in preference to equity for reasons of cost, convenience and control. Debt is a less expensive source, since tax savings are possible on interest paid. Servicing equity, on the other hand, entails payment of tax. The overall cost of capital, therefore, various in an inverse proportion to the debt component in the capital structure of the enterprise. Secondly, debt is relatively more convenient to obtain when needed and to redeem when required. Debt does not also result in any dilution of control over the affairs of the enterprises since leaders do not acquire any voting rights. Lastly, the low-cost debt provides a leverage, which helps achieving a higher rate of return on equity.

There are, however, definite limits to debt financing. Debt involves financial risks. They need to be commensurate with teh business risks. The business risks arise from likely changes in demand for the product, emergence of competition or imposition of controls over prices imports, exports etc. The financial risk grows in proportion to the debt component in the capital structure. Excessive borrowings render the corporate equity riskier and potential investors become more and more reluctant to go in for that equity. It is, therefore, essential to match the two risks and set definite limits to debt financing.

Limits to debt are fixed keeping in mind three interrelated standards, industrial norms, debt servicing capacity and the cash adequacy during recession. Each industry adheres to certain norms of capitalization on the basis of its asset structure and magnitude as well as volatility of its earnings in the long run. It is for this reason that utilities like power industry can afford to employ higher doses of debt. Industries whose earnings are subject to high risks of obsolescence prefer self-financing and go in for a large equity base, which can withstand the shocks. The second factor, namely, the debt servicing capacity is taken as a fraction of the annual cash accruals. Conservative bankerz insist on debt service coverage ranging from 200 to 300 percent. The cash adequacy standard is a variant of debt service capacity standard and is based on cash flows, expected during the recession period. The objective is to ensure the required capacity to service the debt even under the worst circumstances. The three norms together guide the management in deciding on the limits upto which it can seek funds in the form of debt.

It may be relevant to have a closer look at the equity-debt proportion in the capital structure of the central PEs. There are very few instances where the debt is more than the equity and even in these cases, the excess is due to the erosion of net worth because of accumulated deficits. The aggregate position conforms more or less to the age-old policy of the government to maintain a 1:1 ratio for debt and equity.

Acquisition a Short-Term Sources

The current assets held by one enterprise are financed mainly from short-term sources. However, the long-term sources are supposed to provide the margin money and also take care of investments in the core current assets. Bank borrowings in the form of over-drafts or cash are credit suppliers credit and other current liabilities constitute the major sources of short-term finance available to an enterprise. Bank borrowings have become so expensive now-a days that they are exerting a restraining influence on the enterprises. They are trying to manage their current assets more efficiently and are at the same time, looking for alternative and less expensive sources of short-term finance.

The government follows the policy of asking PEs to obtain their credit requirements from the nationalised banks. In those cases where the enterprise is short of margin money, the government extends a guarantee to cover the deficit. When they find it impossible to obtain their total requirements of working capital from the banks, the government provide short-term loans for a specific period.

Investments in Long-Term Assets

The enterprises employ their capital partly in fixed assets and partly in current assets. The financial administrators have to ensure that funds at the disposal of the enterprise are judiciously employed, and that the proposals for further investments are economically feasible areas and justifiable. The investments in fixed assets involve substantial long-term commitments in terms of finance as well as technology. The proposal for each investment is to be, therefore, subjected to a cost benefit analysis.

A professional analyst has a number of techniques at his disposal for carrying out the cost benefit analysis. The following four techniques have found practical applications:

(a) average rate of return

(b) pay back period

(c) internal rate of return (IRR) and

(d) net present value (NPV)

All these techniques help financial administrators in choosing the best project.

Short-term Investments

Major investment decisions may be subject to external pressures on the enterprise. But the decisions on current asset-holdings fall well within the scope of internal management. Investments in Inventory can be regulated to ensure that excess stocks and stock-outs are avoided. Similarly, efficient management of trade credit enables keeping the investments in sundry debtors to the absolute minimum. Better management of cash offers scope for reducing the interest burden on the enterprise.

The techniques of ABC analysis, economic order quantity, reordering level standardisation; value analysis, etc. help managing the current assets more efficiently. The financial administrators coordinate the use of the techniques since they eventually help him manage the fund tied-up in current assets.

Planning System

The planning process in the enterprise includes strategic planning, long-term corporate planning and annual performance budgeting. It also covers economic and financial analysis needed for short-term decisions.

Strategic Planning refers to planning major strategies concerning expansion, diversification, taking up manufacture of new products, entering new markets, etc. The financial administrator plays a crucial role in marshalling the relevant costs and benefits and in advising the management on the long term financial Implications In terms of outlays and resulting cash flows expected. He works closely with the team engaged in the strategic planning process. In fact use of the investment decisions discussed earlier are integral part of strategic planning.

Long Range Corporate Planning is the process of developing a time bound plan for achieving the objectives of an enterprise over a period of five or more years. It takes into account all the on-going activities as well as the new projects being taken up and prepares an integrated total plan for the enterprise as a whole. Here again the financial administrator plays a major role in assimilating the data, appraising the alternatives and developing master budgets and financial forecasts for covering the plan period.

The performance budget is an extension of the corporate plan. It is, prepared in greater detail and sets physical and financial targets for each responsibility centre and builds the efficiency norms into them. The budget thus serves as in instrument of planning as control. The profitability need not necessarily be the guiding index of performance. What is needed is a system for review and target setting for each segment of the enterprise. The Management by Objectives (MBO) may be adopted for formulating and implementing the performance budget. These budgets enable decentralisation of authority and centralisation of control. Budgets also help management by exception.

Operating Decisions

There are very few decisions at the enterprise level, which do not affect its funds. It is therefore; logical for the financial administrators to have a say in those decisions. Leaving aside the investment decisions mentioned earlier the operating decisions cover a wide range of problems such as capacity utilisation, pricing, overtime working, shift-working, product mix credit policy and incentives.

Control Systems

Budgetary control and standard costing systems provide the basis for monitoring enterprise performance at all levels. They introduce a participative element in the target-setting exercise.

The financial administrator is expected to develop an integrated system, which incorporates statutory accounting as well as management accounting systems. The system has to be so designed as to generate data for compiling periodical reports to be sent to the administrative ministry, Finance Ministry and Planning Commission etc. It should also provide information to enterprise managers at all levels about their achievements vis-a-vis plans and targets. These managers need assistance in identifying and analysing cost variance as well as profit variance.

Internal Audit is considered to be an integral part of finance functionin most of the PEs. It is internal appraisal and is mainly concerned with the evaluation of the effectiveness of other managerial controls including systems and procedures. The external auditors rely very much on the internal audit for ensuring the credibility of basis transactions and records.

The financial executive coordinates with statutory auditors in carrying out the external audit once a year. PEs are audited directly by the Comptroller and Auditor General of India (CAG) or by chartered accountants appointed by him as auditors. In the latter case, he has powers to carry out a supplementary test audit. There is an audit board, which coordinates the external audit work in respect of central PEs in India.

Financial Objectives for PEs

PEs are different from private sector enterprises in terms of both the nature and obligations to the nation. The private sector enterprises possess a great deal of clarity in terms of their objective, which is the maximisation of their profitability essentially. PEs are composed of two terms, viz. 'public' and 'enterprise'. By being 'public' these enterprises stand accountable to the government. Their management and ownership also rests with the government on account of this characteristic. The term 'enterprise' means that PEs have to produce certain goods or render certain services at a price resulting in excess of income over expenses which should be duly reflected in the profit and loss account and balance sheet. Further, these enterprises operate in diverse sectors including manufacturing, financial, promotional and welfare activities. There are about 1100 State Level Public Enterprises (SLPEs) run by 25 state governments of the Indian Union and 240 central PEs. However, these enterprises can still have a uniform financial objective which may range from the retention of the net worth to its maximisation implying the fact that enterprises at the bottom of the scale will have to keep their net worth intact whereas enterprises at the other point of the scale can multiply their net worth in a business-like manner. The welfare enterprises engaged in serving the needs of the weaker sections of the society are not suited for profit maximisation. However, in order to maintain their present level of operations and their likely expansion, they must keep their net worth intact. On the other hand, the manufacturing enterprises operating in competitive sectors can maximise their net worth based on the market leads.

Financial Organisation for PEs

Organisation for finance has undergone a radical transformation in PEs with the changes in the environment governing PEs and their structures. The financial organisation has acquired sophistication and complexity with the marketisation and partial privatisation of PEs.

Diagram 1 shows a typical organisation chart of the Financial Management Division in PEs.

Diagram 1

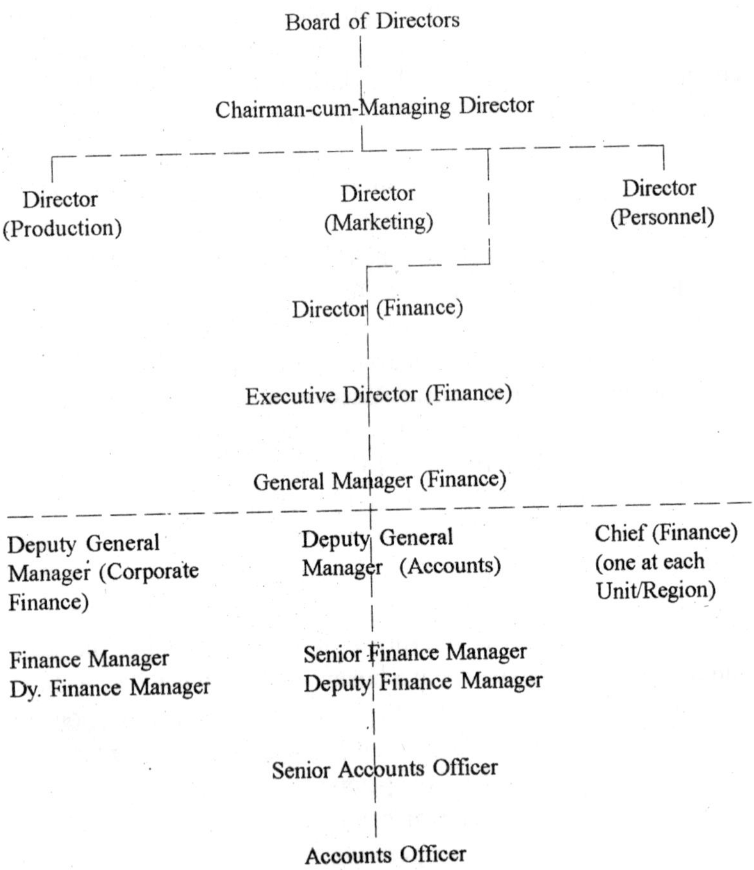

As the diagram shows, the Finance Division is headed normally by the Director (Finance) who holds the board level position. He advises the Chairman-cum-Managing Director (CMD) on all matters pertaining to finance and accounts. He is responsible for formulating and coordinating out the financial plans. He executes a staff function and at the same time happens to be a line authority for the executive in the finance department. He is assisted in his task by Executive Director (Finance) and General Manager (Finance). The Executive Director is assigned some specific tasks besides helping the Director (Finance) in the formulation of financial policy. These may include responsibility for audit and preparation of budget. The General Manager (Finance) is saddled with routine affairs such as the preparation and finalisation of accounts, compilation of budgets, handling of cash credit and arranging corporate finance. In most of the PEs, the Director (Finance) is recruited by the Public Enterprise Selection Board. The earlier convention of deputising the officer from the Finance Ministry or the office of the CAG has been abolished by the government. Diagram 1 shows that in case an enterprise Is, a multi-unit/multi-product concern, the financial organisations provides for a functionary (normally of the level of General Manager) to head this function at the various locations, or product groups.

Investment Management in PEs

Investment proposals for establishment of new units or expansion of new units emanate either from ministries/departments of the government or from the enterprises desiring expansion and growth. The broad nature of investment is determined by the priorities indicated in the National Plan. Individual investment proposals are required to be within the overall programmes outlined in the plan document. The government exercises a measure of control over the size and pattern of investments in the PEs by reserving to itself the power to approve capital outlay exceeding certain financial limits. The government also, exercise control over such investments through the mechanism of scrutiny and approval of the annual capital budgets of the concerned enterprises.

The investment proposals are examined by various agencies of the government including the Projects Appraisal Division of the Planning Commission and the Plan Finance Division from financial, technical, economic and management viability angles. Their relevance to the overall plan objectives, availability of resources, social cost-benefit, etc., is also assessed. All investment proposals costing Rs. 20 crore and above require approval of the government at the highest level after these are cleared by the Public Investment Board. The Public Investment Board constituted with the Secretary (Expenditure) in Ministry of Finance as Chairman. Its other members include Secretary, Planning Commission, Secretary, Department of Economic Affairs, Secretary, Industrial Development, Secretary, Department of Public Enterprises, Secretary to the Prime Minister and Secretary of the Administrative Ministry concerned bringing up the investment proposal before the Board. As per the delegation of financial powers effective from 8.6.1988, the powers of the ministry/departments with integrated finance system, for sanctioning projects/schemes, was enhanced upto Rs. 20 crores but this power can be exercised after following usual Expenditure Finance Committee (EFC) procedure and after obtaining the comments of the Planning Commission and other appraising agencies. Projects costing Rs. 20 crores and above continued to be considered by Public Investment Board, Cabinet Approval is also obtained where expenditure is Rs. 20 crore or more. The powers of the Board of Directors of PEs to sanction capital expenditure were also enhanced in August 1986. As per the revised delegations, the powers of the Board of Directors are as indicated below:

Public Enterprises with Gross Blocks of	*Power to sanction capital expenditure without prior approval of Government*
Less than! Rs. 100 crores	Rs. 5 crores
Between Rs. 100 crores and Rs. 200 crores	Rs. 10 crores
Above Rs. 200 crores	Rs. 20 crores

In addition to the above delegation, Government vide O.M. dated 7.11.1988 and 29.8.1990 have further delegated enhanced powers to Board of Directors of Memoranda of Understanding (MOU) signing companies to incur capital expenditure. As per the revised delegation, it has been decided that in respect of companies signing MOUs and having gross block of over Rs. 200 crores, the power to incur expenditure on additions, modifications and new investments will, be raised from the existing limit of Rs. 20 crores to Rs. 50 crores without the prior approval of the Government and the power to incur expenditure on replacement renewal of assets from the present limit of Rs. 50 crores to 100 crores provided.

(a) the required funds can be found from the internal resources of the company and the expenditure is incurred on schemes included in the capital budget approved by the Government;

(b) new items should have been identified and discussed at the annual plan discussions and outlays provided for; and

(c) for repairs and maintenance, the delegated powers being exercised should be within the framework of a lumpsum provision agreed (to and provided for at the annual plan discussion).

Financing of PEs

There are various sources of financing PEs. These mainly constitute equity and grants received from the government, public participation in equity, borrowings from the open market in the form of public deposits and issue of bonds, foreign investment and cash credit advances.

The government is the main provider of funds to PEs. It finances PEs through equity grants and borrowings. The borrowings are provided at a rate of interest of 14-16 per cent per annum for long-term funding. The equity is provided for long-term funding at no cost. Thus, the equity represents the perpetual interest free capital. To check the misuse of cost free funds, the government has initiated a scheme of divestment of equity in PEs from 1991-92 in which year Rs. 3,000 crore was received from the sale of PE shares through mutual funds. The government's equity in the Central PEs was of the order of Rs. 38,634 crores as on March 1, 1990. The long-term loans provided by the Government to PEs amounted to Rs. 24,585 crores as on the same date. The central government provided about 68 per cent of the total financing needs to these enterprises in 1989-90. The foreign participation in terms of equity and debt amounted to Rs. 14,221 crore as on the same date which measured to about 14 per cent of the total financing needs in 1989-90. The equity and loans provided by the financial institutions amounted to Rs. 5,213 crores as constituting about 5 per cent of the total financing needs as on March 31, 1990. The private participation by way of bonds, equity and public deposits amounted to Rs. 60,496 crores which represented roughly 16 per cent of the total financing needs as on March 31,1990.

The working capital requirement of PEs are generally met through cash credits and advances arranged with the State Bank of India a nationalised banks. The total amount of outstanding cash credit drawn by the central PEs stood at Rs. 13,973 crores as on March 31, 1990. In special cases non-plan loans also are arranged by the central government to some enterprises to meet their working capital requirements. As on 31, March 1990 the Rs. 14.40 crore was due in these enterprises under this head.

Despite the recommendations made- by several expert committees/commissions such as the Krishna Menon Committee (1959), Administrative Reforms Commission (1967) and Committee on Public Undertakings (1971), these enterprises did allow public participation in their equity. The internal financing through generation of internal funds by way of depreciation, write-offs and retained profits constitute another important source of financing PEs. The internal financing is a cost free source of finance. Between 1985-86 and 1989-90 the internal resources generated by these enterprises stood at Rs. 37,677 crores. Not only that the volume of internal generation of resources increased between 1985-86 and 1989-90 from Rs. 5,067 crores to Rs. 10,779 crores, respectively, but the number of PEs generating internal resources also increased from 126 to 150 crores during the same period. The generation of internal resources reduces the dependence of PEs on the government and thereby acts as an important measure of autonomy.

Financial Performance of PEs

As discussed earlier, the productiveness of the financial administration has to be seen in the ultimate financial performance of an enterprise, which has assumed critical importance in the present context of severe resource crunch faced by the Indian economy. The public sector in India contributes 25 per cent to the gross national product of the nation. It holds a position of great strength in several economic activities despite the present move about privatisation. It is expected that PEs in India will double their size in terms of investment from Rs. 3 lakh crore at the end of Seventh Plan to Rs. 6 lakh crore at the end of the Eighth Plan. These enterprises contribute substantially to our foreign trade. About 20 per cent of the foreign trade is transacted through these enterprises.

Table 1 shows that the central PEs with an investment of over Rs. 1,10,000 crores as on March 31, 1991 had earned profits of less than Rs. 3,000 crores. The table also shows that the profitability of the central PEs declined by 40 per cent during 1990-91 over the previous financial year.

Table 1
Profit Status of Central PEs

	Units	1980-81	1983-84	1984-85	1985-86	1986-87	1987-88	1988-89	1989-90	1990-91
1	2	3	4	5	6	7	8	9	10	11
1. Number of running public enterprises	Number	163	201	207	211	214	221	226	233	236
2. Capital employed	Rs. crore	1820-7	29851	36382	42965	51835	55554	67629	84869	101797
3. Turnover	Rs. crore	28635	47272	54784	62360	69088	81271	93137	106069	118355
4. Gross margin profit before depreciation, interest & tax	Rs. crore	2401	5771	7386	8230	9897	11134	13438	16412	18510
5. Depreciation*	Rs. crore	983	2205	2758	2983	3376	4150	4866	5790	7151
6. Gross profit before interest and tax	Rs. crore	1418	3585	4628	5287	0521	8984	8572	10822	11359

1	2	3	4	5	6	7	8	9	10	11
7. Interest	Rs. crore	1399	2086	2529	3115	3420	3595	4167	5329	7539
8. Net Profit before Tax	Rs. crore	19	1480	2099	2172	3101	3389	4405	5293	3820
9. Tax	Rs. crore	222	1239	1190	1000	1330	1329	1411	1504	1452
10. Wet Profit after tax	Rs. crore	-203	240	909	1172	1771	2060	2994	3789	2368
11. Internal Resources generated (Gross)	Rs. crore	1225	3278	4251	5068	6014	6947	8915	10774	11372
12. Met Profit (after tax) to capital employed percent		-1.1	0.8	2.5	2.7	3.4	3.7	4.4	4.5	2.3

* Includes deferred revenue expendiure.

Source: Financial Express, Economic Survey: 1991-92, Bombay, March 1, 1992, p. vii.

Table 2 shows that the position of the departmental PEs was none too good. These enterprises incurred losses continuously.

Table 2
Financial Results of Departmental Commercial Undertakings of States and UTs [Profit (+) / Loss (-)]

	1985-86	*1986-87*	*1987-88*	*1988-89*	*1989-90*	*1990-91*	*1991-92*
1. Depart. Coss. Undertakings							
(i) forest	497.70	516.21	543.69	414.35	540.24	372.46	528.33
(ii) Power projects	-75.04	-93.81	-116.40	-84.19	-34.83	-54.56	-42.98
(iii) Road & Water Tpt. Services	-25.65	-36.59	-110.76	-56.51	-93.21	-75.78	-64.10
(iv) Diary Development	-99.29	-40.45	-43.91	-52.38	-106.99	-72.33	-77.18
(v) Industries	-14.10	-16.46	-20.51	-10.09	-159.56	-112.91	-40.04
(vi) Mines & Minerals	40.06	35.05	27.02	51.83	60.62	60.43	75.26
(vii) Irrigation Projects (Commercial)	-871.60	-1225.95	-1344.50	-1840.79	-1916.85	-2002.63	-2206.66
(viii) Multipurpose River Projects							
2. Profit of Profit making undertakings	537.76	551.26	570.71	466.18	600.86	432.89	603.59
3. Loss of loss making undertakings	-1068.68	-1413.26	-1636.08	-2043.96	-2311.54	-2318.11	-2430.96
4. Net Financial results of department undertakings	-547.92	-862.00	-1065.37	-1577.78	-1710.68	-1885.22	-2430.96

* These do not include State Electricity Boards and Road Transport Corporations.

Source: Financial Express, Economic Survey: 1991-92, Bombay, March 1. 1992, P. vii.

The SLPEs followed suit. According to one estimate, the losses incurred by the SLPEs during the period 1985-86 to 1990-91 amounted to Rs. 14,000 crores. The State Electricity Board, and the State Road Transport Corporations were the major culprits. However, there are PEs which have had an unblemished profit making record. Some of these enterprises include the Oil and Natural Gas Commission, Bharat Heavy Electricals Ltd., Electronics Corporation of India, Air India, Hindustan Petroleum Corporation Ltd., Indian Petro Chemicals Ltd., Indian Oil Corporation Ltd., Indian National Thermal Power Corporation Ltd., Steel Authority of India Ltd., Oil India Ltd., and Bharat Thermal Power Corporation Ltd. The top ten loss making enterprises as on March 31, 1990 included Hindustan Fertiliser Ltd., Fertiliser Corporation of India Ltd., Indian Iron and Steel Company Ltd., Delhi Transport Corporation Ltd., Engineering Projects Ltd., Hindustan Ship Yard Ltd., Hindustan Steel Works Construction Corporation Ltd., Cement Corporation of India Ltd., National Jute Manufacturers Corporation Ltd. and Hindustan Cables Ltd.

The dismal financial performance of PEs has resulted from sub-optimal project planning, under utilisation of capacities, lack of aggressive marketing, poor production and planning and control, unsuitable product mix and over-staffing. Externally, the failure of PEs to manage the environment to their advantage has also contributed a lot to this phenomenon.

An efficient and effective financial administration can turn the corner of the ailing PEs. An important way to overcome this malaise is to resort to the introduction of the OPTIMA (optimum performance through internal management action) in PEs. This will result in the commercialisation, corporatisation, restructuring and privatisation of PEs. PEs will do well to adopt the private sector style of management. Externally, the government–PE Interface needs to be made harmonious. The Introduction of Memorandum of Understanding (MOU) is a right step in this direction.

New Initiatives in the Realm of Financial Administration in PEs

The financial administration in PEs in 1990s is expected to proceed along new lines. In the field of financing, PEs will resort increasingly to capital market. The new instruments such as equity-cum-debenture convertible issues, cumulative convertible preference shares, warrants etc. will find their place in PEs. PEs will make forays in international capital markets. They are likely to get listed on various stock exchanges in the country and their shares will be available for trading. The function of financial administration is expected to acquire participating orientations. The use of electronic data processing systems are likely to replace the hunch driven decisions in the realm of finance administration. The cost of capital is expected to assume the primacy in the area of financial decision making in PEs.

Summing Up

PEs constitute an important segment of the economic system in India. Their contribution to the national economy is phenomenal. Their effective functioning is extremely crucial for the success of the planned economic efforts. The effectiveness of financial administration measured in terms of the profitability points out that these enterprises have lagged far behind the expectations. They can make significant improvements in respect of the three components of financial administration viz., investment , management, financing and checking up on their financial performance. The function of financial administration is undergoing a sea change in PEs. These enterprises have started organising their financial organisation in a business like manner. They have commenced efforts to reduce their dependence on the government through the capital market. They have initiated exercises to review their investment portfolio to weed out non-operating assets. There is a great scope for toning up further the activities pertaining to financial administration in PEs.

Index

G

I

J

K

L

M

N

O

P